The Land and People
of South Africa

PORTRAITS OF THE NATIONS SERIES

THE
LAND AND PEOPLE
OF
SOUTH AFRICA

BY

ALAN PATON

J. B. LIPPINCOTT COMPANY—PHILADELPHIA & NEW YORK

Contents

Other volumes in preparation

The Land and People
of South Africa

1. THE CONTINENT

If you look at the smaller map on page 16 you will know at once what this great mass of land is. It is the continent of Africa, and it has an area of eleven and a half million square miles. From Algiers to Cape Town in a direct line is five thousand miles. From Cape Verde to Cape Guardafui is almost the same.

The Union of South Africa, the country at the southernmost end of the continent, is in area about one twenty-third of the size of the whole. This is the country we are going to visit. It is often called briefly the Union.

But let us first look for a while at the map of Africa. You will see on any detailed map that the African coast is almost unbroken; it has very few bays and inlets, and is therefore poor in harbors. The continent is also poor in navigable rivers. This is because the interior of Africa is a raised plateau, and the coastal regions drop sharply to the sea. You therefore get much beauty of scenery, especially on the eastern coasts, where the drop is steeper than on the west. The rivers run through wonderful panoramas of mountains, hills, cliffs, and valleys, and are full of waterfalls and rapids. After the rains these rivers are swift and turbulent; but they are very uneven in flow, especially in South Africa, which for the greater part gets no winter rain at all. There are very few stretches of flat and well-watered coast, where a central river gathers to itself many tributaries, and flows broadly and quietly to the sea.

It is partly because of this lack of harbors and navigable rivers, and partly because the interior plateau is shut away behind its ramparts, that for hundreds of years Africa was, and even now still is, the least known continent of the earth.

But there were at least two other reasons for this. One was that there was almost no communication between the greater part of Africa and the rest of the world; its peoples had no written language, no vehicles, no roads. Inquisitive Europeans came prying into Africa, but the African himself stayed at home. Another reason for Africa's isolation was its extreme heat and dangerous diseases; those who have read the stories of the early explorers will know how many failed to return. On the Niger, the Congo, and the Nile, in desert, swamp, and forest, they developed unknown fevers, and far from any aid, collapsed and died.

It was inevitable that the white man with his technically advanced culture, should sooner or later try to discover what lay beyond the Mediterranean coasts of Africa, and the vast desert known as the Sahara. Sooner or later he must encounter the African people.

Today the African people are very sensitive to any description which would label them as primitive or simple or backward or childlike. I shall try to avoid any hurtful use of words. The fact is that the white newcomer confronted the African people with a new and fantastic and wonderful and terrifying world. The African stared awe-struck at the ships that came out of the sea, and at the white-skinned men that came out of them. He stared fascinated at mirrors, and his wife was fascinated by new cloths and materials of every color. Their pleasure and admiration they showed with laughter, with uninhibited gestures, with dancing. They did not hide their pleasure, they showed it. White men, unused to such openness and simplicity, found them childlike, and wrote such opinions down.

The African was terrified of gun and rifle. When the first one was fired, he might well have run off into the jungle, to return later with a more uncertain laughter. Every strange achievement of these newcomers was greeted by expressions of wonder and admiration. Nor were these new tools, instruments, ornaments, merely marvelous because they were new; they gave the white man power, and he soon controlled the continent even in places where he had been resisted.

In their turn some of these white men were fascinated by the laughter, the singing, the dancing, the strange innocence of these tribal people, and were filled with admiration for their way of life. There was cruelty, ignorance, superstition enough; but there was something else also, a serene acceptance of custom and convention, a natural obedience to authority, some strange beauty and simplicity of life that civilized man had lost.

You may know that many people have held up African society as an example to inspire and to shame our modern civilization. Comparisons of this kind are helpful up to a point, but not beyond it; for the one overwhelming fact is that, for better or for worse, African society wastes away before modern civilization. Indeed the whole story of Africa is the story of how Western, Christian, technical civilization came to an unknown continent, and changed forever and forever the simplicity of its life. Such a story cannot properly be told or understood by those who are obsessed by the wish that it had not happened, or who are obsessed by the desire to prove that the one way of life was superior to the other. We shall try to avoid both of these obsessions.

As I sit writing here I look out over a wild but beautiful African landscape of great valleys and hills. Through the middle of this scene runs a tarred highway, and automobiles pass up and down continuously. But also traveling the road, mostly on foot, are many Zulu people. The men are for the most part dressed in European clothes, but many of the women wear tribal dress. Some wear a gaily colored cloth over the breasts, but some are bare from the waist up; they are going shopping, to buy goods of which their forefathers had never heard. Down the valley runs another road to the Government clinic; tribal Zulu women are going down the hill to see the doctors there. At the clinic they will meet other Zulu women, qualified nursing sisters in white uniforms. The African people are truly people of two worlds.

Altogether it is a strange scene, this picture of a people in transition.

We shall try to learn more about the people, and about their way of
life, what it was, what it is becoming, what many of them hope it will
be.

So the continent of Africa is opening up, and now more swiftly than
ever before. South African Airways flies to London, and international
airlines fly to Johannesburg. Automobiles travel from Algiers to Cape
Town, though it is still a difficult and often dangerous journey, especially across the Sahara Desert. A motorist crossing these northern
wastes must travel hundreds of miles between gasoline and repair stations, even between water supplies.

To fly from Tunis to Johannesburg is a wonderful experience. From
Tunis to Kano in Nigeria one flies for many hours over a wasteland
in which by night is to be seen no light, by day no road, no vehicle,
no habitation. From Kano to Brazzaville the scene changes, and one
passes over a wonderland of hills, valleys, forests, streams and rivers,
but still with little sign of human activity, certainly not that kind of
activity which is visible from a great height. From Brazzaville to
Johannesburg there is still little sign of human activity until one enters the air over the Union of South Africa. So far we have seen an
occasional road with an occasional vehicle. But now roads, towns, vehicles, farms, dams and railway lines become more visible and numerous; it is clear that human activity of a different and more spectacular
kind is going on there below. And if this last stage of the journey is
made at night, the lights of Johannesburg are a sight not to be forgotten. Strange that one must travel nearly the whole length of the continent to see such a spectacle.

Whether one travels from north to south by automobile or plane,
it is as one approaches the Union of South Africa that the wildness
of the continent increasingly gives way to roads, towns and villages,
telegraph poles, bridges, and buildings of all kinds that are clearly not
the simple buildings of old Africa.

This is because South Africa has been settled by white people from

Europe for three hundred years, and it is technically and industrially the most advanced country in the continent.

We are going to learn more about this country. We are going to learn more about the impact of Western civilization and Western ideas on the African way of life. We are going to learn more about the problems that result from this.

But we are going to have a holiday as well. We are going to enjoy the brilliant sunshine of South Africa, which escapes the great heat of the interior of the continent. We are going to visit gold mines and diamond mines, to visit one of the tribal reserves, to see the greatest waterfall of the world, and to travel in the vast Kruger National Park, where we shall see lion, giraffe, elephant, hippopotamus, crocodile, cheetah, zebra, eland, kudu, impala, and many other animals, moving about their natural habitat without fear of man.

2. THE UNION OF SOUTH AFRICA

The Union of South Africa is made up of four provinces, the Cape of Good Hope, the Orange Free State, the Transvaal, and Natal. How these four provinces came together to form the Union of South Africa, we shall learn later.

The Province of the Cape of Good Hope is a little larger than Texas, the Transvaal is the size of Nevada, the Orange Free State is the size of the State of New York, and Natal the size of Indiana.

The two small pockets which you see on the map, are called Basutoland and Swaziland, and do not form part of the Union, nor does the Bechuanaland Protectorate, which lies on the northern borders. These countries are respectively, as you may guess, the homes of the Basuto, the Swazi, and the Bechuana people, and are ruled direct from Britain; but the Union of South Africa is a sovereign state, and rules itself, and belongs by choice to the British Commonwealth of Nations.

Now suppose that we prepare for our journey through South Africa. Where shall we begin, and what shall we do?

Most of our American visitors arrive today by air, at the large modern airport between Johannesburg and Pretoria. But, nevertheless, I am going to suppose that you arrive at Cape Town by ship. I want you to see South Africa as it was first seen by the sailors from Europe. And what is more, I then want to take you overland to Johannesburg, because it was by that route that South Africa was opened up to the world. If you travel by this route yourselves, it will help you to understand our history better.

If you will look again at the map of South Africa, you will see the route that we are going to follow. You will land at Cape Town, and I shall take you by train to Kimberley, the diamond city, and then to Johannesburg, the center of the world's greatest gold-mining industry. We shall spend some time there, and make at least three journeys out of the city.

The first journey will be by automobile to the Kruger National Park, in the Eastern Transvaal.

The second will be by automobile to Pretoria, the administrative capital of South Africa.

The third will be by air to the Victoria Falls, which, as you will see, are not in the Union at all. They are in Rhodesia, but we could not bring you all this way to South Africa, and then fail to take you to the Falls.

Then from Johannesburg we shall go to Durban, the largest city of Natal, returning overland to Cape Town. This route will take us into the large tribal area known as the Transkei, and through some of the most magnificent mountain passes in Africa.

When will be the best time to visit South Africa? In fact, it is pleasant to be there at any time of the year. Some of the summer days can be very warm, but we are spared the great heat of other parts of Africa. Many people, both visitors and South Africans, love to stride about in the hot brilliant sun, and, if they are white, to burn themselves chocolate on the bathing beaches. Our summers are, on the whole, not oppressive; South Africa is not a land of steaming jungles, but a country of wide and open spaces, covered by grass and scrub rather than forest. This open country is called the veld, which is pronounced like the word *felt;* and its summer weather, though often hotter, is less oppressive than the summers of New York and Washington. Remember that the greater part of South Africa is not situated in the tropics at all.

Nevertheless, I am going to suggest that you come in our winter months. This is because the Kruger Park lies partly in the tropics, in hot, low country below the escarpment of the interior plateau. Malaria is still common there, and because of that the Park is closed in the summer, except for a small portion in the south.

You must get used to the fact that our winter months are not the same as yours. Our winter falls in June, July, and August, and this is the best time to visit both the Victoria Falls and the Kruger Park.

But do not bring the winter clothes that you would wear in America. You are not likely to see any snow, except on the mountains. Bring a good winter coat, because it can be cold in the Transvaal, especially in Johannesburg, which is nearly six thousand feet above the sea. But in the Park you will be most comfortable in shirt and shorts made of the lightest material that you can find, if you are a boy; and if you are a girl you may wear the same, or some light summer frock.

And bring your cameras, for in the Park you will be able to take the most exciting pictures, of wild animals standing or lying only a few feet from the car in which you are traveling. These pictures will make you the envy of your friends back at home, and will silence those who find it hard to believe your stories.

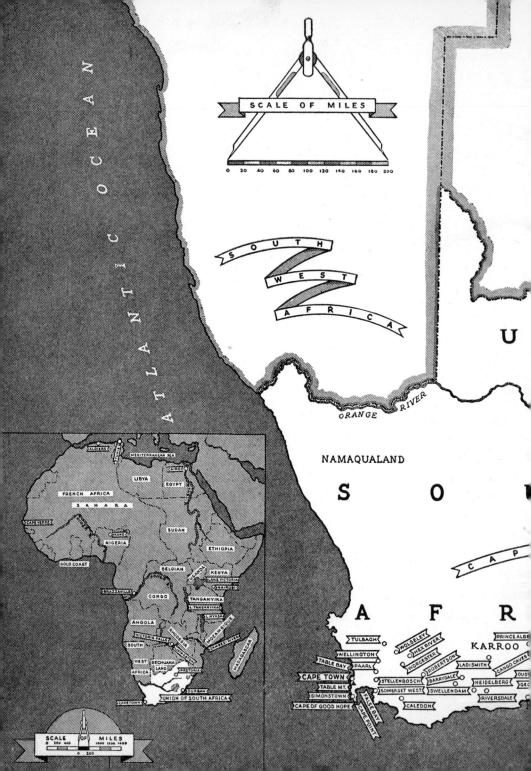

SCALE OF MILES

0   20   40   60   80   100   120   140   160   180   200

ATLANTIC OCEAN

S O U T H   W E S T   A F R I C A

U

ORANGE   RIVER

NAMAQUALAND

S O U

C A P E

A F R

MEDITERRANEAN SEA

ALGIERS

CAIRO

LIBYA

EGYPT

FRENCH AFRICA

S A H A R A

CAPE VERDE

SUDAN

NIGERIA

ETHIOPIA

GOLD COAST

BELGIAN

KENYA

UGANDA

LAKE VICTORIA

BRAZZAVILLE

CONGO

TANGANYIKA

TANGANYIKA

L. NYASA

ANGOLA

RHODESIA

MOZAMBIQUE

MADAGASCAR

VICTORIA FALLS

ZAMBESI RIVER

LIVINGSTONE

SOUTH

BECHUANA

WEST

LAND

PRETORIA

AFRICA

DURBAN

CAPETOWN

UNION OF SOUTH AFRICA

KARROO

TULBAGH

WOLSELEY

HEX RIVER

PRINCE ALBERT

WELLINGTON

WORCESTER

TABLE BAY

PAARL

ROBERTSON

LADISMITH

CANGO CAVES

OUDT

CAPE TOWN

STELLENBOSCH

BARRYDALE

HEIDELBERG

GEO

TABLE MT.

SOMERSET WEST

SWELLENDAM

SIMONSTOWN

FALSE BAY

RIVERSDALE

CAPE OF GOOD HOPE

CAPE POINT

CALEDON

SCALE   OF   MILES

0   200   400   1000   1200   1400

0   200

3. THE CAPE PENINSULA

If you come to South Africa by sea, you will land at Cape Town, which lies at the foot of Table Mountain. This mountain stands 3,600 feet out of the sea, and has a long flat top like a table. Sometimes, when the sky is otherwise clear, a thin layer of dense white cloud lies on top of the mountain, and this is called the Tablecloth.

According to the great historian Herodotus, Egyptian sailors circumnavigated the continent of Africa six hundred years before Christ. But it was not until A.D. 1486 that any human being is recorded as having seen the great mountain from the sea. This human being was Bartholomew Diaz, who rounded the Cape in such fierce weather that his sailors called it the Cape of Storms; but when King John of Portugal heard of the discovery, he realized its importance, and renamed the Cape, calling it the Cape of Good Hope, which it remains to this day. Some authorities say, however, that it was Diaz himself who, making his return voyage in happier weather, and being bound for home, gave it this happier name. The famous English sailor, Sir Francis Drake, called it "the fairest Cape in the whole circumference of the earth."

The Cape is three hundred years old, as history goes. It was in 1652 that van Riebeeck landed there with the first Dutchmen to establish a refreshment station for the ships of the Dutch East India Company on their way to the countries of the East, and we can see his statue at the foot of Adderley Street, Cape Town. The Cape is not like any other part of South Africa. It is made different by its mountain scenery, its vineyards, and its climate; and also by its historical age, for the rest of the Union of South Africa is only just over a hundred years old, as history goes.

We must spend a few days in Cape Town before we travel on. It is a city of two thirds of a million people, and there is a great deal to see. One of the things which cannot be missed is the expedition to Cape Point, along one of the most magnificent mountain and ocean drives in the world. The mountains here fall straight into the sea, and the road runs hundreds of feet above the Atlantic Ocean. Then it descends, and runs along the lonely and beautiful tongue of the Cape Peninsula, to the lighthouse at Cape Point. Here will be seen wild baboons, which can be fed but must not be played with. Hundreds of feet below are the blue clear waters of the Atlantic, in which can be seen the long black shapes of sharks.

In fact, you will see two oceans. As you look south, the waters on your right are those of the Atlantic, which washes the eastern coasts of America. On your left is the Indian Ocean, which washes the western coasts of Australia; its waters are warm and pleasant, while those of the Atlantic are cold.

The motor coach now leaves Cape Point, and returns north to Cape Town along the coast of False Bay. Here you pass the harbor of Simonstown, which is the home of the African Squadron of the British Navy; then the seaside resorts of Fish Hoek, Kalk Bay, St. James, and finally Muizenberg, which has the finest bathing beach in South Africa. Over on the other side of False Bay can be seen the wall of the Hottentots Holland Mountains, sometimes clear, sometimes faint, always majestic.

Soon we are back again under the mountains of Cape Town, running along the de Waal Drive. This part of the city still breathes the spirit of Cecil John Rhodes, who was the millionaire Prime Minister of the Cape Colony in pre-Union days. Here is Groote Schuur, which means Great Barn, the home which was built for him by Herbert Baker, the great architect. Rhodes gave this to be the home of the Prime Ministers of the Union of South Africa, and the Prime Minister lives there now.

Here are also the fine buildings of the University of Cape Town, the magnificent hospital, and the Rhodes Memorial itself; few buildings in the world have such magnificent sites, and such a majestic background.

Nor must we fail to visit some of the old Dutch houses. They are impossible to describe, except to mention their white walls, their gables, their shuttered windows, their oaks and vineyards. They rejoice in names like Vergelegen, Rhone, Meerlust, Groot Constantia, La Gratitude, Perel Vallei, Stellenberg, and Alphen. They are of their kind perfection. Groot Constantia is easily reached. It was the home of Governor Simon van der Stel, and was finished in 1685. After being destroyed by fire, it was faithfully rebuilt by the Union Government, and is open to visitors. Most of these old houses had slave quarters, and these can still be seen; but of these slaves we shall hear more when we come to discuss South African history.

We are back in Cape Town again, and we must not neglect to visit the Castle, which is the oldest building in South Africa. Here are grim reminders of how prisoners were treated in those far-off days. Then there is the Koopmans de Wet Museum, which is full of magnificent old Dutch furniture, and the Martin Melck House, both picturesque old buildings. Nor should we fail to visit the site in Adderley Street, nor the market behind the Post Office where many flowers, cultivated and wild, are offered for sale. We must try also to see the Municipal Botanical Gardens in Cape Town, and the National Botanic Garden at Kirstenbosch, both with magnificent mountain backgrounds. There are also two well-known art collections in Cape Town, the National Art Gallery and the Michaelis Gallery; and next to the Municipal Botanical Gardens is to be found the South African Museum. Cape Town prides itself on being the most mature and cultured city of South Africa.

The Dutch Reformed Church in Adderley Street is the oldest standing church in South Africa, having been commenced in 1699. The Lutheran Church in Strand Street is a fine old building, and was commenced in 1780. There are Anglican and Catholic cathedrals; and to remind us that Cape Town is a cosmopolitan city, there are the mosques, where the Malays worship, the descendants of the slaves brought to South Africa in the early days.

There are many more places to see, but you must not omit to visit the Houses of Parliament, where the laws of the Union are made. The Union is a small country, but its laws are of interest to the whole world, largely because they are now mainly concerned with the strict separation of all the races that inhabit South Africa.

Now we must climb Table Mountain, by foot if we are feeling energetic, by cableway if we are not. The view from the mountaintop is magnificent, and it will enable you to understand more clearly the geography of Cape Town. For this city, that lies almost at the very south of the continent of Africa, has a most puzzling geography until you realize that it faces north, not south at all.

4. THE PEOPLE OF CAPE TOWN

A visitor to Cape Town would certainly be impressed by the natural beauties of the Peninsula, but he would be equally impressed by the diversity of the city's peoples. They are of many races and colors. There are thousands of white people in the streets, and thousands of people who are of every color from near-white to black. Most of these near-white people are the Cape Colored people; but the darker ones, the brown and the black, are the Bantu people, the Africans, who did not originally belong to this part of South Africa, but have come here to work.

The Cape Colored people are a mixture of many bloods, of the Malay slaves, of white settler and sailor, of the Hottentots. When the Dutch first came to the Cape in 1652, it was inhabited by Hottentots. They were easily conquered; some fled further inland, and some stayed to work for the white people. But they were not very hard-working, and the colonists imported slaves, mostly Malays. So emerged the Cape Coloreds.

They are in general a cheerful and friendly people; they range in color from white to dark brown, in possessions from modest wealth to bitter poverty, in conduct from uprightness to criminality, in status from doctor and headmaster to lowly laborer. They have long regarded themselves as a separate people, ever since a changing custom, and then finally a law, forbade further intermixture.

Many of them have the ordinary vote, but a colored man cannot himself be elected to Parliament. Even now the white Parliament is debating whether this ordinary vote, that is, this vote on the common roll, should be changed for a separate vote on a separate colored roll. These matters are very complex, and we shall talk about them further when you have seen more of the country. In the meantime let us observe all that we can.

You will not only have noticed several races and colors but you will have heard several languages. Two of these languages will have forced themselves on your attention, for they appear together on every public notice. One is a language you know well; it is English, the language of Britain and North America. It is also the language of what are called, for want of a shorter name, the white English-speaking South Africans. It is one of the official languages of the Union of South Africa.

The other official language of the Union is Afrikaans, the language of the white Afrikaans-speaking South Africans; but they have a shorter name—they are called the Afrikaners. These are the descendants of the Dutch people who came to the Cape with van Riebeeck in 1652, and of the French and Germans who later joined them. They also have a certain amount of English, Scottish, and Irish blood, but in general the English-speaking and the Afrikaans-speaking have remained quite separate peoples. Nevertheless the race of a white South African cannot now always be told from his surname; you may meet

Afrikaners called McGregor, Gilfillan, Robertson, Harrison, just as you may meet English people called Potgieter, Kriel, and Hattingh.

This cleavage of the white people of South Africa into two distinct language groups is something you will understand better as you travel on. There are separate newspapers, separate schools and universities, separate churches, separate societies and clubs of all kinds. Just how far this separateness goes is something that you must try to observe for yourself.

You will see that English and Afrikaans appear together on every public notice. Sometimes English is above, sometimes below; sometimes on the left, sometimes on the right. You will observe that on some postage stamps both languages appear together, on others the language alternates from stamp to stamp; if you are a stamp collector, you must collect such stamps in unseparated pairs. South Africa is what is called a bilingual country, and the greatest care is taken to see that the languages are treated with scrupulous equality.

These bilingual public signs and notices announce many things, but you cannot help observing how many of them announce that certain rooms, offices, and public counters are for Europeans only, and others are for non-Europeans only. By Europeans is meant white people, not merely people whose forefathers came from Europe. If you are a white American, for example, you must go to the counter for Europeans, not that for non-Europeans. In the Afrikaans notices there is no such confusion; the notice says *Slegs Blankes* or *Slegs Nieblankes,* which means only whites or only nonwhites.

You will have observed that all the guests in your hotel are white, that all the patrons in the restaurants are white, that if you go to a barber's shop or a beauty parlor, all the customers are white. You will, however, notice that in the public transport buses there are people of all colors; this is not usual in South Africa, but still prevails in Cape Town; indeed some white people, especially some of those who visit the Cape from other provinces, protest against it. Again you will notice that in the local trains there are coaches reserved for Europeans only, but that the other coaches are open to all. This last arrangement has only come about in the last few years, but there are still white people who object to this separation arrangement, and who always travel in the open coaches.

In the streets of course there is no such physical separation, nor could there easily be. All kinds and colors of people move about together, and preserve that kind of impersonal good manners which street crowds possess anywhere. If you stand at some busy corner in the city, and listen to the languages spoken, you will notice for yourself that the white people speak either English or Afrikaans; you will hear that the colored people, the people of mixed race, speak mainly Afrikaans, though you will sometimes hear them speaking English. The darker people, the Bantu or Africans, though many can speak English and Afrikaans, will probably be speaking quite other languages that you will not understand at all. These are the languages of Africa, the languages of the Bantu tribes. They are not much heard in the Cape, but we shall visit parts of South Africa where they are the only languages spoken.

Maybe it is very confusing to you. But one thing will become clear. The separation between the English-speaking and the Afrikaans-speaking is largely a separation of custom and culture, though it can also be effected by law, as in the Transvaal schools. But the separation between white and nonwhite is much greater.

If you were a colored American, it would be very difficult for you to visit South Africa, even painful. It would be almost impossible, and certainly painful, for you to come in a party containing white Americans. It would be almost impossible if you came in a party containing only colored Americans. If you came to visit white South Africans you had met in America, you would have to be protected from pain and embarrassment; your friends would no doubt have prepared you for this, but you would not be able to see the country in a natural and easy way.

You might, as a colored American, think that you could take it all as a great adventure, that you could easily endure the embarrassment for the sake of seeing this country, of which colored people all over the world have heard so much. But you would have to be an exceptional person to succeed in your adventure. In most colored people the pain and resentment would climb and climb in their throats, until they became afraid, perhaps not of the country, but of what was happening inside themselves.

It is time we left Cape Town; there is so much traveling ahead of us. But this being the winter month of June, we must go to the famous ground at Newlands, to see a Rugby football match. This is a faster game than soccer, and very different from your own American football. Rugby football came from England, but the Afrikaners have made it their own game. It is one of the elements of South African culture that is equally shared in and treasured by both English-speaking and Afrikaans-speaking South Africans.

Cricket is our summer game, and also came from England, but so far it has not been widely adopted by Afrikaners.

It would, I think, be quite interesting if I gave you the names of those white South Africans who recently represented their country at Rugby football and cricket respectively.

Rugby Football 1951-2		*Cricket 1953-4*
Viviers	Dannhauser	McGlew
Ochse	Barnard	Westcott
Fry	du Rand	Cheetham
Lategan	Muller	Funston
Saunders		Endean
Brewis		Watkins
Du Toit		van Ryneveld
Koch		Waite
Delport		Tayfield
Bekker		Murray
van Wyk		Adcock

It suddenly occurred to me, however, that you are so used to a great diversity of names in America, that you might not at first glance notice the marked difference between these two lists. So I must point out to you that the names of the cricket team are almost all names from Britain, whereas the majority of the names of the Rugby team came from France, Germany, and Holland. In America today such a difference would be probably coincidental, but in South Africa it is racial and cultural. You would find that most of the cricketers were English-speaking and most of the Rugby footballers were Afrikaans-speaking.

By the way, all white South Africans who represent their country are called *Springboks*. The springbok is a graceful African antelope.

Now that you have been introduced to the people and city, Cape Town, let us commence our South African travels, by going to Kimberley tomorrow in a South African train.

5. THE FIRST JOURNEY

All railways in South Africa belong to the same owners, and the owners are the South African people. The railways are called simply, the SAR, or the South African Railways; and in Afrikaans, the SAS, or the Suid-afrikaanse Spoorweë.

Our trains will look a bit small to American eyes; that is chiefly because our gauge is three feet six inches, as compared with the American four feet eight and a half inches. The American gauge permits American engineers to build wider and higher and therefore more luxurious trains, and it permits trains to travel faster and more comfortably.

But we are proud of our trains nevertheless. We decided to use a gauge of three feet six inches because we had to travel long distances through sparsely occupied country; also because a narrower gauge required less excavation and tunneling, especially when climbing the escarpments from the coastal regions to the interior plateau. Every important route in South Africa has to climb these escarpments, for the important routes in South Africa all follow the same recipe—they run from the harbors to Johannesburg.

All harbors in southern Africa lie in the Union of South Africa, except Lourenço Marques, which lies in the Portuguese territory of Mozambique. All these routes must climb or descend the escarpment, and must often pass through mountain country of considerable difficulty. One of these ascents you are going to make today.

The platform from which the train is to leave is crowded with people. There is no great concourse here such as you find in America, before whose gates you say goodbye to your friends, and then descend alone to your platform. Here your friends all come with you, to say cheerio or *tot siens,* which is the Afrikaans for till we meet again.

Let us look at the passenger lists and see where we are booked. The train looks very smart, you must agree. As we climb aboard, you will note that the passageway or corridor does not run down the center of the coach as it does in the States. Here it runs down the side, and the coach is cut off into many rooms called compartments. Our compartments will strike you as being more comfortable than your day coaches, and more private and comfortable than your ordinary sleepers, though less private than your roomettes.

In the first-class compartment are accommodated three people. The two upper bunks are folded into the wall during the day, and we should have a pleasant journey. If we had traveled by the famous Blue Train, we should have had greater luxury, including air-conditioning; but air-conditioning is not really a necessity in South Africa, which does not experience great extremes of heat and cold. I must warn you though about the smuts from the engine; if you want to keep the windows open, you are sure to get one or two specks in your eyes.

But the warning bells are sounding, the guard is waving his flag, the engine driver blows his whistle. We are off on our first journey into Africa; one cannot help feeling a certain excitement over that.

Gathering speed we pass through Woodstock, Salt River, and Maitland, and cross the Cape Flats, the sandy tract connecting the Cape Peninsula with the mainland. Soon we are passing through orchards and vineyards lying below the mountains. On our left, as we run through Paarl, are the wine cellars of the KWV, the largest in the world; on our right are the fantastic peaks of the Drakenstein. Through this beautiful countryside the train progresses at a fair speed, past Wellington and its jam factories, past Tulbagh Road and on to Wolseley, where we are summoned to lunch by the musical tones of the steward's gong. We make our way down the swaying corridors to the dining car, and study the bilingual menu, on which if we are lucky we shall find some traditional Afrikaner dishes.

We are still at the foot of mountains. Worcester is eight hundred feet above sea level, but we must ascend another 2,400 feet in the next thirty miles. During this ascent we shall get some magnificent views of the Hex River Valley. We are in fact leaving the fertile mountain valleys of the Cape, and are climbing on to the interior plateau, which at places attains an altitude of six thousand feet.

This part of South Africa is called the Karroo. Nothing could be less like the beautiful country we have just left. Yet people who live on the Karroo, and especially those who were born there and have now left it, go into raptures over its beauty. And many who have never seen it before are fascinated by its solitude, by its stony flat-topped hills called *koppies,* by the colors of its fantastic rocks. Over this seemingly barren plain, we shall travel all afternoon and most of the night; I say seemingly barren, because these desolate wastes can also be transformed by one good rain. Much of the Karroo is covered by short tough scrub that withstands drought; and this scrub country is one of the best sheep areas of the world.

The afternoon is drawing to a close and maybe we shall see a real Karroo sunset. A sunset on these plains can be indescribably magnificent. The dust particles in the crystal-clear atmosphere refract the sun's rays, to splash the skies with wild and splendid colors, changing from minute to minute, lasting and deepening long after the sun has gone. And then let us ask for one thing more, and that is the radiance of a waxing moon, pouring down its silver light on this unending plain.

And now after a good dinner, let us go to bed. The Cape Colored attendants will come along the corridors with sealed bags containing clean sheets, pillows, and blankets. It is already turning cold, but it will be much colder in the night, when we climb to 4,500 feet. There is a heater in the compartment that will help to keep us warm.

Places like Rhenosterkop, Nelspoort, Kromrivier, Three Sisters, De Aar, and Oranjerivier, will pass us in the night. The Oranjerivier, which means the Orange River, is South Africa's biggest river, but in this dry season of the year it is often no more than a chain of stagnant pools. As for the other places, they are not much more than railway stations, and are very like one another; although the Karroo may have a harsh grandeur of its own, that is certainly not true of its human habitations. I am sorry though that you could not see the Three Sisters. They are three of the strange hills in which the Karroo abounds, and truly look like three nuns.

While we sleep, the character of the plain will change. It will still be harsh and dry, and possess no local or immediate beauty. But its vegetation will become more marked, a kind of thorny scrub reaching here and there the dimensions of a tree. I believe that this kind of country rejoices in the poetic name of acacia savannah, but do not jump out of bed on that account.

The steward will waken you early, because we reach Kimberley at six o'clock in the morning.

6. DIAMONDS AND OTHER TREASURES

It happened to me often in the United States that when I told people I came from Johannesburg, they replied, "That's where the diamonds come from." But, in fact, it is gold that comes from Johannesburg; diamonds come from Kimberley, the town we are now visiting. It is not a big place; its population of all races is sixty thousand. But from this place more than any other have come the diamonds of the world.

A diamond, as you probably know, is a crystalline form of carbon, and a close relation of the soot in your chimney and the lead in your pencil. But this particular form of carbon has been made by the gigantic internal pressures of the earth; it has taken on a crystalline quality, it is one of the hardest substances in nature, and it is able to reflect light with blinding brilliancy. Diamonds have an intrinsic commercial value, but they have a much higher value as precious stones; and why they should have, I do not know. I suppose it just is because men give them this value. And women too of course.

Now the same pressures that formed diamonds also spewed them up to the surface, through funnels called pipes or fissures. Over the ages a process of weathering and erosion took place, especially in South Africa, which is geologically one of the oldest of countries. Thus much diamondiferous material was taken down by rivers to the sea, and many diamonds, being heavy stones, were left in old watercourses. These are called alluvial diamonds. They were found in fabulous numbers at the mouth of the Orange River during this century, and had not the Union Government stepped in to control the area, the diamond market—and Kimberley—would have collapsed. Similar discoveries have been made all along the arid coasts of Southwest Africa, and also in Central Africa, in the country of Tanganyika, so it can be seen that the future of Kimberley is a very uncertain one; indeed if diamonds were not a monopoly, Kimberley, and perhaps even diamonds themselves, would have no future at all.

In 1866 a trader called O'Reilly called at the farm of a Mr. van Niekerk near Hopetown. There he was shown a collection of beautiful stones, which the farmer called Orange River stones. One of these O'Reilly at once knew to be a diamond, and he took it away to show to the authorities. Not long after another stone, later known as the Star of South Africa, was picked up and sold for seventy thousand dollars. From all over the world there was a rush of people to the Diggings, as they called them.

Owing to its color the diamond-bearing rock is called blue ground. The rock is hauled to the surface, and taken to the crushing plant, where it is reduced to a particle size of one and a quarter inches, and in this crushing process most of the diamonds are released.

This crushed ore is now taken to rotary washing pans. The ore enters the pan at a tangent, and is carried along by a stream of slime and water called puddle. This suspension of slime increases the density of the water, so that the stream is able to keep the diamonds in motion, but does not allow them to come too near the surface. The upper layers of water continually overflow, but the lower layers, with their precious contents, are removed from time to time through a door in the wall of the rotary pan.

By this process ninety-eight per cent of the ore is removed; it is called tailings. The remaining two per cent is to be treated further.

The remainder is now circulated in what is called a Separatory Cone. In this cone is water containing an iron alloy powder, which again has the effect of making the water dense. Again the lighter particles float off, and the heavier sink.

The third step is the grease table, a table covered with a layer of petroleum jelly, which has an affinity for diamonds. The whole table is vibrated electrically along the line of feed, but the vibrations are so small and fast as to be hardly perceptible.

The final product is now removed from the table and cleaned of all grease, the last picking being made by hand. From approximately ten thousand tons of ore, which is handled daily by all this machinery and all these men, one pound weight of stones has been produced, that is, one part in twenty million.* Yet this one pound weight will pay for all the machinery and all the men, even though a high percentage may be suitable for industrial use only.

You may well ask why all this labor must be performed to recover one pound weight of diamonds, when such a weight can be picked up much more easily on the western coasts of Africa. But the truth is, I do not know.

Let me tell you one more interesting fact. When the diamonds have been finally removed, a fine mineral concentrate is left, consisting mainly of ilmenite. This is sold to golf courses in the more arid parts of the Union, where it is impossible to grow grass to make a green. This gravel is too heavy to be blown away, and too fine to be troublesome to play.

The early days of Kimberley were rough and exciting. Fortune seekers streamed into the Diggings, with a generous proportion of crooks and scoundrels. It was not an easy life, but there was always the hope of a big discovery. It was a gambler's atmosphere; men worked hard, drank hard, lived hard.

The area where they found the diamonds was easy to work at first. But the diggings grew deeper and deeper. There were ten thousand men working there, looking feverishly for the small hard stones that could make a man's fortune. Soon the area of their activities began to look like a great crater in the ground; it was roughly circular, and had a circumference of a mile, and a diameter of 1,500 feet. But the dangerous thing about it was its depth, which was over four hundred feet, and continually increasing.

* The Union Castle Yearbook says one part in thirty-five million.

It was called the Big Hole, and thousands of men worked and looked like ants at the bottom of it, each gang on its own piece of ground. Each bucket of ground had to be carried by wires out of the hole. Earth crashed down ton by ton on unfortunate claims, and their unfortunate owners had to move it all before they could continue. When rain fell in that semidesert region, it fell in good measure, and flooded the hole. Men fought and quarreled, and were killed by falling rock. It was more like a Bedlam than a great mining undertaking. A mining committee was set up but the problems defeated it.

This chaos was finally brought to order by Cecil John Rhodes, that strange and tragic genius of South Africa. He came to Kimberley at eighteen, and eventually decided to control it all. Thus the famous company of De Beers was founded, whose mines you have today been visiting. About Cecil John Rhodes we shall hear again, for he played an important part in our history. Yet today hardly anything remains of his memory but his money.

But we must not close our visit without going to the De Beers head office in the city. It is said that the stones they keep there are worth a million pounds (nearly three million dollars); they will let you see a fraction of that amount. They will show you rare stones and common ones, they will explain how diamonds are best cut, and they will keep an eye on you most courteously and unobtrusively.

Then out into the street for a short walk to the second great treasure of Kimberley, the Duggan-Cronin Bantu Gallery.

Here we shall find a superb collection of photographs of the people of the African tribes of this part of the continent. Over twenty-five years ago a young mine supervisor, Mr. A. Duggan-Cronin, was struck by the beauty of the adornments and the bodies of his laborers, when at the end of the week's labor, they washed themselves, and amongst the alien sights and sounds of the white man's city, put on their tribal dress and so briefly went back home. But he was struck by something else too: that during their brief make-believe, they were no longer laborers but men, able to shut out from mind the fantastic business on which they were engaged, and the drab world in which they worked, so that there returned to their faces that strange compounded look of pride and innocence that lives in tribal eyes.

So fascinated was he by this, and by the kind of places which could breed such men, that he used every holiday that he could claim or beg, and went with them into their own remote countries, photographing their rulers and parents and wives and children, their young and their old, their warriors and their doctors, their brides and bridegrooms, their rites and ceremonies, many of which had never before been seen by white eyes, and many of which will never be seen again, for the world has no longer place for such simplicities.

Encouraged by his employers, the De Beers company, Mr. Duggan-Cronin built up a unique collection, going as far afield as Angola, Bechuanaland, Mozambique, and the Rhodesias in search of subjects. Here in his gallery are over three thousand photographs, to interest and delight all who come to see them, and to preserve for us the beauties of a world that has all but passed away.

I have already told you that the technical civilization of the West (what is often called "white" civilization) has been so powerful, its demands so alien and its material rewards so glittering, its diversity of goods so attractive, that the tribal ways of life have wasted away before it. It does not profit to decide which was better and which was worse; we must accept that it has so happened.

Elsewhere in our journeys we shall see the new kind of life that the African city dweller has now to lead, in some instances showing wonderful powers of adaptation, in others showing the fierceness and sometimes the tragedy of the struggle to adapt and to survive. Often we shall sharply remember the simplicity of bearing and the serenity of gaze that are portrayed in these photographs, and we shall certainly understand more fully and clearly the massive changes and difficult problems that were made by the coming of the white man to Africa.

7. THE HIGHVELD

As we leave Kimberley in the early morning, we notice a railway line breaking off to the left. This is the line to Barkly West, Postmasburg, and Lohathla. It runs into a countryside still more dry and desertlike, but rich in mineral wealth. Barkly West is the center of the River Diggings, where alluvial diamonds are found, rich deposits often being found between the river boulders. Postmasburg and Lohathla are centers of great manganese deposits.

You will notice that Barkly West is an English name, and Postmasburg an Afrikaans one. Lohathla is a Sechuana word, this being the language of the Bechuana people. This diversity of place names you will find throughout South Africa.

Between Warrenton and Fourteen Streams we cross the Vaal River. *Vaal* is an Afrikaans word, meaning grayish or ashen. It is from this river that the Province of the Transvaal, in which we soon shall be, gets its name.

The Vaal is the most important river in South Africa, more important than the Orange, whose tributary it is. It feeds the great Witwatersrand, Johannesburg and many other cities and towns, with water; and one day will probably feed Pretoria too. But meantime towns are growing up along its own banks, and great industries are being established there. Its flow of water is more reliable than that of the Orange, and very seldom in the rainless months does it threaten to waste away. In flood it is a terrible river, with a majesty frightening beyond words. It menaces man, town, and countryside, and pours its sullen flood into the Orange. If the Orange is in flood, too, which is very possible, it becomes one of the world's great rivers, hurls itself over the Great Aughrabies Falls (which alas we shall not see), and pours South Africa's precious water and soil into the Atlantic Ocean, discoloring it for a hundred miles.

But this waste, and to a large extent this danger, is being brought to an end. The violence of the Vaal is being curbed by vast dams that at their making inundate hundreds of square miles of the countryside. By the time the flood waters have passed over these placid areas, and reach the great walls, their turbulence has been lost. But the problem of the precious soil still awaits solution.

Some experts think that eventually most of the people of South Africa will live along the Vaal and the Orange, in this countryside through which we are now passing, because there will not be enough water for them to live anywhere else. You will not see in South Africa anything like the inland lakes, both great and small, to which you are accustomed in America. There is not one natural lake of any size in the entire country. Of course some Americans think that we South Africans are the proud possessors of Lake Victoria Nyanza, Lake Tanganyika, and Lake Nyasa. But when you return, you will be able to tell them out of your superior knowledge that the nearest of these great lakes is more than a thousand miles away from our northern borders.

No, South Africa is on the whole a dry country, but you will see, looking out of the window of the train, that we are now leaving the desertlike regions, and are entering the flat grass country of the Western Transvaal. We are in fact on what is called the Highveld. It is winter, now, and the veld is in its winter colors. It is seen to be true that the beauty of South Africa lies in color, light, and space, rather than in any particular beauty of valley, field, or tree. In fact, when looked at with too analytical eyes, it often appears unlovely and harsh.

We are now five thousand feet above the sea. As we go into lunch, we are only about a hundred miles from Johannesburg. We have passed out of the richest diamond fields in the world into the richest gold fields. This hundred-mile string of mines and towns and cities is called the Reef, and this word reef means a gold-bearing vein or lode. Soon we shall catch a glimpse of our first mine dumps, those flat-topped white hills which are the most striking features of the region in which we shall spend the next few days. Now do not think me too much of a schoolmaster if we recapitulate something of what we have seen so far.

The population of South Africa is about twelve and a half million people, but it is clear that very few of them live on the vast plain over which we have traveled these many hours. The plain is almost treeless, and the trees it has are tough and stunted. It is almost waterless, and its greatest river, the Orange, hardly runs in winter; but its greatest tributary, the Vaal, with its dams, stores a vast amount of water. Characteristic of this plain are the flat ridges called *koppies*, and it experiences hot summers and cold winters, though nothing like as cold as your own. The winter day itself, if there is no wind blowing, is sunny and warm, and there is no greater pleasure after a cold morning's work indoors than to take one's lunch outside and to eat it in the sunshine. But the winter nights are cold, often thirty to forty degrees Fahrenheit colder than the day. When the sun nears the horizon, it is time to get back indoors.

This plain through which we have passed is in part an agricultural country, but much more a pastoral one. But the word pastoral must be understood in its South African sense; there are no pastures, no meadows and fields, except where there are dams that can be used for irrigation. The cattle live on the scrub, and the farms have to be very large to support a reasonable number of beasts. Therefore farmhouses are few and far between, and sometimes no house can be seen for miles. The country is very similar to Texas and Colorado, and bears no resemblance to the rich lands of Iowa, and still less to the fields and meadows of England.

If you have seen farm laborers, you will have noticed that as you leave the Cape, there are fewer and fewer Cape Colored people, and more and more Africans These farm laborers are on the whole a poor and backward people.

Nor must you be disappointed if you have seen few of the African tribesmen of whom there were such beautiful photographs in the Duggan-Cronin Gallery at Kimberley.

The African or native inhabitants of the Union number about eight and a half millions, and they can be divided into three roughly equal groups of Africans. One group lives in the cities, and these earn their livelihood mainly as domestic servants and employees in factories, though the number of teachers, doctors, nurses, policemen, and so on, is increasing. Another group of Africans lives in the reserves, tracts of land which were set aside for them by the conquering white men as they trekked farther and farther north from the Cape; many of these still lead a tribal life, and it is they who appear in the Duggan-Cronin photographs. The members of the third group work as farm laborers on the white man's farms, and it is they that you will have seen from the train. Their earnings from their labor are in kind rather than cash, and they are poorly dressed, and clearly have no great possessions.

The white people of the plain through which we have passed are overwhelmingly Afrikaans-speaking. They are nearly all farmers; the Afrikaans word for farmer is *Boer,* and they often called themselves Boers, though it is not quite polite for an English-speaking person to do the same in English.

And there is your first mine dump, glistening in the sun. That tall structure is called the headgear; it stands above the deep vertical shaft that goes down thousands of feet into the earth; the interior plateau is here five thousand feet above sea level, but in the deepest mines the shaft goes another five thousand feet below sea level.

The mine dump that you see is still in the making. You will see that an endless chain of trucks, or coco-pans as they are called, is being hauled to the summit, where the pulverized ore will be unloaded.

Over there you will see another kind of dump, of more regular shape. That is the slimes-dam. To it is led the slime from which the gold-bearing solution has been filtered. The liquid part of the slime evaporates, and the solid part raises the level of the dump another few inches. These slimes-dams can be dangerous unless they are properly controlled. A heavy rain can fill them with water and cause them to burst, and because of their height above the ground, they can endanger life and property. Their contents, moreover, are poisonous, and can kill stock and vegetation.

There is still gold left in these dumps; in fact all the dumps of the Reef put together contain a fortune, but it would cost a fortune to extract it. There is at least one dump in Johannesburg where a prospector is trying to recover gold; but this would be possible only on one of the older dumps, for as the years have passed, the gold-refining process has become more and more efficient.

Some people find the dumps beautiful. Painters paint them and photographers photograph them. In that way they are like the hills of the Karroo. Of themselves they have no particular beauty, but taken in the large, in a confusion of giant condensers and skyscrapers and headgears and pylons, under pale dawns and fiery sunsets, under the dark skies of night, they make the beauty of Johannesburg. Yet not even the most devoted artist likes them when the wind is blowing; the fine sand lifts off them, and eddies down into the streets, filtering into shops and houses, into people's eyes, into sandwiches, into basins and baths. Yet the sight of these dumps is much the same to the returning Transvaaler as the sight of the Statue of Liberty is to the returning American. Beauty is in the eyes of the beholder.

There can be no doubt now that we are approaching a great city. The desolate plain is behind you, and you are drawing near to Johannesburg. It is the central city of a great string of towns that lie along the Golden Reef, that have brought wealth and poverty, skyscrapers and slums, war and bitterness, but always life and excitement, to that pastoral quietness which was once South Africa.

8. JOHANNESBURG

We are entering Park Station, which is what everyone calls it, though that name is no longer to be found in the railway books, or on the nameboards, which all say Johannesburg. This is the biggest and most modern railway station in all Africa, though it does not compare with the two great terminals of New York. For the time being we say goodbye, or *tot siens,* to the South African Railways, which have brought us safely and comfortably to the busiest center in Southern Africa.

We emerge from the station into Eloff Street, which is the main street of the city. You will see at once that Johannesburg, which has about a million inhabitants, strongly resembles American cities of its size. Tall buildings, busy traffic, hurrying pedestrians, a sense of urgency and hustle. Central Johannesburg has no pretensions to beauty; it is seventy years old, and has been built and rebuilt more than once in its short life, but everybody was apparently so busy seeking fortunes that no one had time to pay any attention to the planning of the city. It contains some beautiful buildings, but not one beautiful street. In the fairly extensive business center of the city there are only two open pieces of ground, and both are small. Much better provision was made in the newer parts of Johannesburg, but in the central part of the city the chance is perhaps forever lost.

Let us go to Escom House, which is the home of the Electricity Supply Commission; it is the tallest building in Johannesburg, and many think it is the most handsome. It has twenty-one stories, or seventeen if you do not count the top towerlike portion, and rises to a height of two hundred and thirty-six feet; armed with this information you can compare it with the tallest building in your own city.

From the top of Escom House we shall get a good view of Johannesburg. First and foremost we shall realize again that Johannesburg is the heart of the gold-mining industry; everywhere we turn, except to the north, we shall see mining headgear, dumps, and slimes-dams. Two hundred and thirty-six feet below us we can see cars in the streets, and human beings going like ants about their business. There is nothing very remarkable in that; it is a commonplace in any city. But thousands of feet below these streets, other vehicles are moving about their own underground streets, and thousands of human beings are going about their work of loosening the precious ore so that it can be taken up to the surface and its valuable contents extracted.

Johannesburg is a city belonging to our Western, industrial, technical civilization. It is in Africa, it is true, but it is not in the wild Africa or the dark Africa of legend and history. Johannesburg has all the characteristics of your own larger cities; there are air-conditioned cinemas, big department stores, swift transport, radios, jukeboxes, neon lighting, expensive restaurants. Many of its modern gadgets and fittings come from the United States; so do most of its films, and most of its popular music. If you look at the cars in the streets, you will note that all the bigger ones came from America. The American influence on our life and culture is considerable, and if you observe carefully, you may be able to gauge just how considerable it is.

I have already told you that our summer game is cricket, and our winter game Rugby football; both these games came from England. Baseball was introduced from America many years ago, but is not yet a serious rival. Soccer, or association football, came from England, and is very popular, but hardly seems likely to oust Rugby football as the national game. Hockey, tennis, and golf are universal, the first two having come to us from England, and the last from Scotland. Basketball is a popular game for girls' schools, and came from the United States. *Jukskei,* which is the Afrikaans word for yokeskey, the vertical pin in an ox yoke, is a very popular Afrikaans game, but does not seriously compete with any of the games mentioned above. It will be seen that the European influence on our games is overwhelmingly strong.

The nonwhite people of South Africa, especially those who are drawn into the Western orbit, notably in the cities, are also becoming a game-playing people. But it is soccer that has become their great game; indeed it seems to be the most exportable game in the world. The elite of African town dwellers, the teachers, doctors, nurses, and so on, play tennis, but only at their own nonwhite clubs. The Indian people are keen on cricket, the Africans less so. But the future of all these games amongst nonwhite people is unpredictable; so much depends on their own economic and social advance, and their own tastes.

You will find that white clubs are exclusively for white players; friendly matches are sometimes played between some white and some nonwhite teams, but these are unofficial, not official. When you hear that South Africa has beaten Australia in a cricket match, that always means white South Africa. But if you were to hear that South Africa had beaten Nigeria, or that South Africa had beaten the Gold Coast, that would certainly mean nonwhite South Africa. Such matches have not yet taken place, and if you study the map of the continent, you will see how far away these places are.

Sport is often said to be one of the best solvents of race and color prejudice, but if you are to understand South Africa at all, you must learn that even in the world of sport the color lines are very sharply drawn. For example, South Africa and New Zealand are the two strongest Rugby-playing countries in the world; now New Zealand has a considerable number of colored citizens called the Maoris. When South Africa visits New Zealand, she plays against all New Zealand; but when New Zealand visits South Africa, the Maoris are left at home. When, however, New Zealand visits England, Scotland, and Wales, she does not need to observe this color bar. White South Africans are madly enthusiastic about Rugby, and especially about playing New Zealand, and it would be a great shock to them if the New Zealanders decided that they could not visit South Africa any longer under these circumstances.

Indeed, it is hard to say what the future of sport in this country will be, if the white people maintain their rigid color bars. It is for example impossible for a nonwhite player to gain a place in a team representing South Africa, in any kind of sport whatever. Even at this moment the International Lawn Tennis Federation is arguing with South Africa over this very matter. Sooner or later it seems to me that every international sporting body will have to reject South Africa as a participant so long as she maintains a color bar. I for one do not understand how a country like New Zealand can consent to a color bar when she visits South Africa; I should have thought she would have had more pride.

However, I did not intend to go off at this tangent; let us return at once to our discussion on American influence in South Africa.

In our tall buildings, we use lifts, not elevators, and so it seems likely to remain. We go to the post office for the post, not the mail. We used to listen to the wireless, but we are now listening more and more to the radio. Most of us still go to the bioscope, but more and more of us are going to the cinema. Okay, (or O.K.), is now a word in English, Afrikaans, Tamil, Hindustani, Zulu, Sesuto, and many other African languages. Some South African mothers call their children honey, and some South African girls call a boy a guy. We still say "I don't feel very well," but we shall know what you mean if you say "I don't feel so good." And if you say "Did I like it, or did I?" we shall understand quite well what you mean.

When you spell colour, color, and humour, humor, we shall know that you are not making a mistake. But if you say you are going to stay in Johannesburg from Monday thru Thursday, or even Monday through Thursday, you will probably have to explain what you mean, because we always say from Monday to Thursday. And be careful, too; if you want to book accommodation—that is reserve a room—for June 7, 1954, don't write 6/7/1954, because that means July 6, 1954. You write Month/Day/Year, and we write Day/Month/Year, and both practices are so deeply entrenched that it will not help to argue which is more sensible.

We are grateful for American influence on South African dress, especially men's clothes. What a delight it is to have got rid of studs, and of shirts with detachable collars, and of garters for holding up socks; these American-made elastic-topped socks are comfortable and tidy. And what a joy to have shed that piece of armor-plate that was called an evening-dress shirt. However, we still wince a little when an elderly American tourist visits us in a shirt sporting comic strips, or the headlines of the American newspapers. We are more conservative than Americans, and less conservative than Englishmen. We use one another's Christian names far more freely and far sooner than we used to, but we are still far behind the Americans in this respect, especially those of us who are older.

The Americans have also influenced our food habits. We use more fruits and fruit juices than we used to; we are more adventurous in introducing fruits into vegetable salads; our consumption of breakfast cereals increases yearly. For some reason we are not great water drinkers; you may have to ask for your iced water. Tea and coffee are our national drinks, coffee being on the whole more used by Afrikaans-speaking people, and tea more used by English-speaking people, also increasingly by nonwhite South Africans. Places of refreshment are indeed often called in English tearooms, but in Afrikaans *koffie-kamers*.

Chewing gum is little used in South Africa; and indeed to see some respectable American in a film, watching a tennis match or a horse race or an accident, alternately chewing and forgetting to chew in his excitement, is enough to send a South African audience into fits of laughter.

As for humor, we are again situated between the Americans and the British. We are thus able to enjoy American humor, with its quips and wisecracks, and at the same time those British comedy films which seem to many of us to be subtle, and to many Americans to be dull. Yet broadness and subtlety are not really the respective characteristics of these kinds of humor, as a study of American and British comics will soon show.

We South Africans of all races have a great respect for America. This is partly because you are so rich, and partly because you are so powerful; but it is also partly because those of us who have visited you, know you to be a warm and generous people.

And now let us walk back through the evening streets to our hotel. The warm day is over, and it is suddenly cold, but of course we are 5,750 feet above the sea. Tomorrow we shall be thousands of feet below it, for we are going to go down a gold mine.

9. A GOLD MINE

Our visit to the gold mine will make clear to you that gold mining is an industry involving tremendous capital. Today it needs about thirty million dollars to take a bare piece of South African veld and to turn it into a producing gold mine; that is to say, you must spend about thirty million dollars before you get your first dollar returned. You had better first be certain that there is gold underneath.

The gold in many mines is found in a tilted reef, which runs at an angle, say forty degrees, to the horizontal veld above. Therefore if you follow it from where it outcrops, you will find that after a certain distance it has plunged deep into the earth. Some of our gold mines are already over nine thousand feet deep. The temperature increases as one goes deeper into the earth, and the general conditions are so abnormal as to require much scientific investigation into the possibility of working at such great depths. Engineers and scientists are of the opinion, however, that mining can now be continued to a depth of twelve thousand feet.

At one time the threat of silicosis or miner's phthisis hung over every man who worked underground. This was an affection of the lungs, caused by breathing in particles of dust, but its incidence has been greatly reduced in recent years. Another risk that is run by the miner is that of falls of rock, which may of course be an immediate cause of death, or may entomb miners and shut them off from escape to the main shaft. Our great mining organizations have a magnificent record of achievement in the fields of medicine and accident prevention. Luckily the gold mine is not subject to the terrible danger that always threatens the coal mine, the dreaded gas explosion.

The underground workings of the gold mine are extensive. Its operations are simple; the gold-bearing reef is loosened, mainly with the use of dynamite, it is loaded into trucks, taken to the main shaft, and hoisted by cage to the surface, where the gold will be extracted. But these operations are simple, and have been made simple, only because of the patience, industry, and ingenuity of man.

It is a fine morning, and we are passing through typical mining districts. We pass headgear, mine dumps, slimes-dams, rows of white mine employees' cottages, and the larger compound for African miners. Frequently we see groups of these miners crossing the roads, either going on shift or coming off shift, with their metal helmets, their lamps, their tremendous boots. Because of these frequent crossings, there are frequent notices to motorists which say Beware of Natives, and photographs of these notices have been published more than once in influential American newspapers and periodicals, to show how terrible the race situation is. But they have nothing to do with the race situation at all, and their publication as such shows ignorance or something worse.

Here we are at the mine, and they are waiting for us. There are many buildings on the surface, but we shall visit them when we come up again. They show us the powerful and truly immense machinery that is used to take down men, vehicles, equipment, tools, into the heart of the mine. There is the largest winding drum in the world, with its miles of strong steel cable snaking down into the dark throat of the shaft—there is a giant windlass, with its tremendous driving wheel, its axle as thick as a large tree trunk. There is a giant ventilating fan, said to be the largest in the world, that keeps the air fresh in all the shafts and passages of this tremendous mine. It also helps to keep the air cool, and to purify it of the dangerous dust that fills the air; this dust is the result of the dynamite explosions which loosen the ore.

Now they are calling us to come and change our clothes. The boys will be supplied with khaki shirts and khaki shorts, which are a schoolboy's workaday costume in South Africa. But all can keep their own clothes on if they want to. Both girls and boys will be given oilskin hats and light coats, which will be welcome in the wetter and colder parts of the mine. No rubber soles may be worn, as they are dangerous on wet surfaces. But we can borrow gumboots, and if we like, we can give back the oilskin hat, and take a real miner's helmet.

Visitors now get into the cage that stands at the top of the shaft. You cannot help a feeling that is a mixture of nervousness and excitement, very like the feeling one gets waiting for one's first plane to take off. After all, down below us there are thousands upon thousands of feet of empty space. And they aren't going to descend carefully either—there is a sway, a sickening lurch, a sick feeling in the stomach and perhaps in the heart too, and we are off. The cage seems to be descending at a breakneck speed; actually it is traveling at only three thousand feet a minute. Note the brilliantly lit stations that we flash past; some are the entrances to horizontal shafts that lead to the Reef itself, some are pumping stations or first-aid stations. It is an odd and an exciting journey; and suddenly with another sickening lurch, it comes to an end. Your stomach, that was just becoming acclimatized, wonders what is happening now. The cage staggers to a halt. You are four thousand feet down, having done it in just over a minute. Your eardrums protest against this swift change of status, but you hold your nose and blow them back to normal. When you are all out of the cage, it clangs to, and drops out of view, probably to do another four thousand feet. As for yourself, you are hurried into another cage that is going to take you down to six thousand feet, but this time along a sloping shaft. How fantastic, we are now below sea level! We have lost in a couple of minutes all that altitude that the train took a couple of days to gain, often struggling and groaning to accomplish an especially severe gradient.

Here waiting for us is a miniature electric locomotive, and a train of wagons; in these we shall ride to the place where miners are actually mining. It is noisy down here. All around us is the rumble of the coco-pan trains, either going to be filled, or already full of the ore of the golden reef. Let us follow this empty train; it is returning to the rock face where the miners are working. Now you can hear the stuttering of the steel rock drills; you have often seen such drills aboveground, when workmen are digging up a street. That is where they are working, in a place called a stope.

This stope, as you can see, is little more than a rough shelf running off the corridor. We had better light our lamps, for we are now in a dark and undeveloped portion of the mine. It is from these dark and undeveloped portions that the gold comes; the rest of the mine, with its shafts and its galleries, its trains and its brilliant lights, its great main shaft going up to the surface, its massive machinery and its buildings and its dumps, its compounds and its housing schemes, even its palatial offices in the city of Johannesburg, all of this exists for, and is kept in existence by, the ore that comes out of these dark stopes.

Now we must get on our hands and knees, and crawl along, so low is the roof. If you have claustrophobic tendencies, you had better go back to the shaft and wait for us. There are eight thousand feet of earth and rock above you, and you must not get too imaginative about it. The rest of us will crawl on, guided by the tunnel and by the sound of the drilling. See, there they are, a white miner and his black assistants! See how their bare bodies shine, how the sweat pours down face and neck and arms! One of the black men is lying under the drill, guiding it with his foot, and drilling holes in the rock wall. In these holes will be placed charges of dynamite, and when all of us have retired to a safe distance, the charges will be detonated. Then the rock will come tumbling down, and the whole mine will seem to shake and tremble, filling us again with that feeling that is a compound of excitement and fear.

It is a bit disappointing to see no gold shining in the walls about us, or glistening from the ore that is being taken to the surface. But many more things have to be done before we shall see any sign of recognizable gold.

Listen to the white miner; he is talking Afrikaans to our guide. The great majority of white miners are Afrikaners. The black miners come from everywhere, from the Union itself, from Basutoland, Bechuanaland, Swaziland, from Rhodesia, Mozambique, Nyasaland, Tanganyika. Most of these Africans are still tribal in their culture, and come from places less affected by European influence; but they have admitted gold mining into their tribal pattern. Some will come a dozen or more times to the mines during their lifetimes, each time for a year at least.

These laborers live in large mine compounds, and great attention is paid to their health and recreation. At the beginning of the century, the death rate from disease was 30 in every thousand, but in 1952 it was only 2.07 per thousand. Their tribal dancing is encouraged, and it is one of the sights of one's lifetime to see a great tribal dance; the whole earth shakes with the stamp of warriors' feet, and the air trembles with their fierce and barbaric song, beautiful yet strange, like nothing else that you have ever heard.

But for all that, the compound system is a bad one. It separates husbands from their wives for long periods, and fathers from their children. It can be defended on several grounds; one argument is that no mining concern could afford to provide housing for the families of all its workers; another argument is that the miners would not want their families to come to Johannesburg anyway, and to leave the peace and shelter of their tribal home. These arguments are quite well founded, but it does not alter the fact that unnatural lives breed unnatural vices, and that the African miner in Johannesburg is an easy prey to the lures of the great city. Nor does it alter the fact that the social life of the reserves is kept at a low level by the frequent absences of its men.

It is true—and you will see many proofs of it—that the mines look after their labor well. It is also true that the mines would perish if they could not get labor so cheap. We need not blame the mines; we must blame a society that puts money before men.

But it is time we went back to the surface, to see what has become of that trainload of ore.

Back at the surface we have a shower, put on our own clothes again, and are ready to see what happens to the ore. At the top of the shaft it is tipped into a giant ever-shaking sieve, where the larger pieces are separated from the smaller. The larger pieces pass along a conveyor belt to the crushing plant, and then join the smaller pieces in the stamp mill. The uproar is so deafening that it is impossible to hear a word, but it is easy to understand what is happening. The ore is being crushed by giant hammers each weighing a ton, and it then passes into the tube mills where it is ground to a wet mass called pulp.

The pulp is then passed over stationary tables covered with corduroy, and a great deal of the gold is deposited on the corduroy in the form of a pyritic concentrate. This concentrate is recovered by washing the corduroy at regular intervals.

The concentrate is now amalgamated with mercury, and the amalgam is smelted and cast into gold bars, which are sent to the Rand Refinery, which purifies the metal still further, until it is 99½ per cent pure gold.

They show us one of these bars, and tell us jokingly that we can have one if we can carry it away. The problem is, however, not so much one of weight, as of the difficulty of getting any kind of grip on the bar. It is said that a visitor with a gigantic hand once succeeded in doing so, but I do not know if there is any truth in that. If it were, he was holding over twenty thousand dollars in his hand.

The Union of South Africa produces nearly half of the world's gold. Canada comes second, and produces about one sixth of the total, followed by the U.S.S.R. and the U.S.A., which each produce about one thirteenth of the total.

In 1952 the Union produced gold to the value of nearly £150,000,000 (over $400,000,000), diamonds and coal coming second amongst the minerals, each with about one tenth of that amount. But the importance of the gold industry was far greater than that; it gave employment to forty thousand white people and over a quarter of a million Africans; it was responsible, directly and indirectly, for great industrial development; towns declined or prospered according to the state of the mines near them; the railways, the shipping companies, the aviation companies, all depended on the mines for a considerable percentage of their custom.

In fact, it was often said that South Africa's whole prosperity was built on gold. That is less true than it used to be, for we are rapidly developing our secondary industry. But it was the gold industry that started it; indeed it started many things. The discovery of gold (and diamonds) brought to an end South Africa's long period of isolation from the world. It was the cause of greater cities, faster railways, better roads. Although the gold industry, as I have explained to you, keeps tribal life going, it has indirectly done more to destroy it than any other single factor. Gold was the cause of our bitterest war, from whose bitterness we are by no means recovered. It has been the source of great fortunes and the most generous benefactions. For better or for worse, for richer or for poorer, gold has had an incalculable influence on South African history and life.

The gold industry is nevertheless passing through an anxious time. The United States of America buys most of our gold at thirty-five dollars an ounce. Most of this gold is sent to America in bars, and is put into the ground again at Fort Knox. This is an interesting, fascinating, mysterious fact, but you will have to get someone else to explain it to you. Now every other commodity has risen steadily in price, but the United States will not pay more for gold. Faced by rising prices in every other direction, the gold-mining industry has kept going only by the use of economy and more and more efficient methods.

It has often been said that the gold industry was dying, that gold is only a mineral, and all mineral wealth comes to an end. Pessimists have said that ten years, twenty years, thirty years, would see the end of gold, and that grass would grow in the streets of Johannesburg.

But in 1946 great new gold fields were discovered in the Orange Free State; their wealth is computed to be as great as the wealth of the Witwatersrand. What is more, the gold content of the ore is generally higher, though the technical difficulties are expected to be greater.

But not only gold continues to keep our country going. Uranium was discovered to be a component of the gold-bearing ores, and South Africa is at the moment the greatest uranium producer also. For a long time men have been afraid of our dependence on gold, which they called a doubtful asset, but now we find ourselves endowed with a mineral which is bound up with the whole future of the human race.

10. THE NEW AFRICA

Well, are you ready for a day's tour of the city? And did you all feel the big earth tremor last night? It is one of the biggest that they have had in Johannesburg for some years, and set all the cups and saucers rattling. These tremors are felt every day in the Johannesburg area, and are due to shifts in the earth's crust (magnified I believe by the extensive mining operations). Johannesburgers are used to them, and only comment when the tremor is very severe.

It is my intention today to take you all on a bus tour of the city, and especially to the suburbs where people live. On our way we shall pass many fine and important buildings; if you are particularly interested in any of them, and want to see what goes on inside them, you will be able to visit them on your free days.

Behind the fine City Hall which you have already seen, is one of the city's few open spaces, and here stands the fine Library Building. This you must visit if you do nothing else, for it contains the Africana Museum (that is, the museum of all things African), and this will help you to understand, in an interesting and fascinating way, more of the history of South Africa.

We turn left and soon come to the famous Corner House, the Headquarters of the Transvaal Chamber of Mines, of its kind the most important organization in the world. The Chamber was at one time reputed to be a maker and breaker of governments, but today it is Afrikaner Nationalism which plays that role. Near the Corner House is the famous Stock Exchange, which has seen the excitement of famous gold strikes and the ruin and tragedy of collapsing markets. Here in April 1946 was the greatest excitement of all, when it was announced that a borehole sample taken from the new Free State gold fields was one hundred times richer than the average Witwatersrand sample. This next imposing building is the headquarters of Anglo-American, one of the greatest and richest of the mining groups.

Then comes another tremendous building, the Johannesburg Magistrates' Courts, where a great number of magistrates deal with the crime of the city. A South African magistrate would be called a judge in America, but here the title judge is reserved for the judicial officers of the superior courts.

Many imposing buildings are being erected in this very old part of Johannesburg, which is called Ferreiratown. But the place itself is not far removed from a slum. Great riches and great poverty exist side by side in this golden city; that is true of course of many cities, but it is truer of Johannesburg than of any other city in the world. Many of our tourists never see the parts of the city that you are going to see today, but it is important that you should see them if you are trying to understand the land and people of South Africa.

From Ferreiratown we pass on to Fordsburg, another very old part of Johannesburg. Here you will see many kinds of people, both white and colored. Many of these colored people are Cape Colored, and have been attracted to Johannesburg by stories of its riches. From Fordsburg we pass to Vrededorp, which means the village of peace; here again you will see signs of great poverty, and representatives of many races. Vrededorp has the reputation of being the worst slum in South Africa, but it is merely the best known.

This mixing of races is strongly disapproved by the present Government of the Union, and it has passed the Group Areas Act, which will define residential areas throughout the Union of South Africa, and make it impossible for members of one race to live or to own property in areas other than their own. As you already know, members of the white race may not marry nonwhite people; and it is the Government's intention to register the entire population, and to define the race of every person, so that racial intermixture may come to an end. Many white South Africans, and in particular many Government supporters, view with abhorrence the intermixing that takes place in countries like Brazil, and are determined that it will not take place in South Africa. They are determined that every race in the Union shall have its own customs and its own way of life, live in its own areas, marry its own kind, have its own schools, pursue its own happiness, all under a wise but firm white leadership. This is a tremendous program, presenting tremendous difficulties, arousing tremendous interest over the whole world, not least in the United States of America; and therefore we must return to discuss it later.

From Vrededorp we strike out to the west, passing through the white residential areas of Brixton, Mayfair West, and Westdene. These are working men's suburbs, and you will hear more Afrikaans spoken here than any other language.

But now the character of the city changes. On the left is the municipal location called Western Native Township, on the right is the freehold township called Sophiatown, in which areas live about sixty thousand African people. Let us first visit the Western Native Township, which location we have received permission to enter. Such permission is obtained from the Municipality, and no white person may enter a location without this permission. You will note that we enter through a gateway, where there is a policeman on duty, and you will note that the whole location is surrounded by a high fence of iron palings. You should, however, be very careful not to draw the wrong conclusions from this; you should ask one of the officials why it should be so, and because you are an American, he will not think it an odd question.

This location of Western Native Township is one of the older locations. When it was built it was an achievement. The houses are small, but they were meant to be let at a rental within the means of the African inhabitants of Johannesburg. Each house has its garden, and there are a number of trees. The whole effect is one of orderliness and pleasantness. These houses and plots belong to the Municipality of Johannesburg, and no African may own any such property here. That is one of the things that is difficult to understand, because a property-owning people is always more stable, more law-abiding, and less vulnerable to the wiles of troublemakers. Naturally the decision to sell these houses and plots would mean that these locations would be more complicated to administer; so this was a case of putting bookkeeping before men. But nowadays it is more than that, for the present Government regards the town-dwelling African as a visitor to the white man's cities, who comes there to work and to earn money, but whose real home is in the reserves, those tracts of land that were set apart for his tribe, when it yielded to the all-conquering white man trekking up from the Cape.

We now leave Western Native Township, but not before we have looked inside one of the houses. It belongs to an African man who is earning three pounds (say nine dollars) a week. We are welcomed by a pleasant-looking woman; the house and its possessions are humble, but it looks proud and clean. The housewife is pleased by our admiration, and especially by the notice we take of her children. She tells us their names and ages, and of the work that her husband does in the city. When we leave she thanks us for coming. She stands at the door and waves to us as we clamber into the bus. We drive away, proud of belonging to the human race.

We now cross the road to Sophiatown, which has no gates or fences. It is a freehold township, where Africans have been able to buy land and build houses. There is nothing rich or palatial here, but there are many solid and well-built houses. Here, if we had time, we could meet African doctors, teachers, businessmen, newspaper men; there are no millionaires, not even any very rich men, but there are many men of substance. They are the forerunners of the new kind of African, and the new kind of Africa. They are the people who have come from the tribal life, and have adapted themselves bravely and intelligently to the industrial city.

But there is another kind of new African, too. There at the corner are six young African boys, of sixteen, seventeen years of age, squatting on the ground, playing at some game of cards. They look at us watchfully, and we can hear the clink of money, but when we reach them, there is no money to be seen. They continue to play; when we speak to them, they answer sullenly; watching them is a girl of sixteen, whose dress is clean enough, but whose undergarment reveals her filthiness. They are uncomfortable while we stand there, and they try to conceal it by talking more loudly amongst themselves. And it could happen, as we turn the corner, that there is an argument, a curse, the flashing of a knife, and someone is dead.

Did you smell something stronger, more pungent than tobacco, while we stood watching the card players. That is the smell of the burning leaf or seed of the plant called *insangu* or *dagga,* and it is closely related to your marihuana. When smoked, it sometimes produces serious changes in behavior; the intelligent become stupid, the docile become aggressive, the reliable become irresponsible. Insangu is a common

element in the patterns of juvenile delinquency, as are the knife, the
gambling, the dirty girl friend.

I do not want to lecture you on juvenile delinquency, which is also
known in your own country. But I wish to point out one important
factor in the situation which is peculiar to South Africa. Much of
this delinquency, this idleness, this sullenness, this quick recourse to
the knife, is due to the fact that the number of occupations open to
these boys is very restricted. They cannot become garage mechanics
or skilled mine workers or municipal bus drivers or trainmen or brick-
layers. White artisans in many trades refuse to open these trades to
African apprentices.

The industrialization of South Africa, with the opening up of many
factories, has helped a great deal to improve the situation. It has
created new occupations which have meant work for many African
boys. The factories have helped to break down, to some extent, the
evil color bar, by which men of one color deny to men of another the
right to do certain kinds of work.

I may add here that those who believe in the total separation of the
races find here a strong argument. How will a black boy get justice,
they ask, so long as he remains in a white society? Is it not better
that he should have his own society where he may do any work that
he is able to do?

These important questions we must talk about later.

In the early days of Johannesburg, these nonwhite areas that we
are now visiting were on the fringe of the city, and about five miles
from its center. But now white suburbs have surrounded them. It is
therefore the intention of the Government to move these sixty thousand African people to an area about ten miles from the center of the
city, and thus to create homogeneous racial areas, in accordance with
the intention of the Group Areas Act. But further, in accordance with
the proposition that the African's home is in the reserves, no African
will be able to own either land or house in the new area; thus those who
had freehold rights in Sophiatown will lose them.

Naturally there is great opposition to these proposals amongst Africans. Those who owned land and houses in Sophiatown are shocked. Africans might feel so strongly that they would defy the law, and offer resistance, even passively. But under the new Criminal Law Amendment Act, the penalties for resisting, and for inciting others to resist, have been greatly increased. Under these circumstances it is no easy matter to disobey the law.

We now leave Sophiatown, and pass to Newclare, which is one of the worst slums in Johannesburg, and a place with a most unsavory reputation. I once put down an Indian passenger at one of these corners, and left him to walk thirty yards to his friend's house; but in those thirty yards he was robbed of all his possessions. He did not resist, for had he resisted, he might easily have lost his life as well.

It is a relief to quit Newclare and to enter Orlando, the giant suburb where live some eighty thousand Africans. It is not a beautiful place, but time and nature and the occupants are softening its ugly regularity. Luckily South Africa is a vast country, and each house in Orlando has its little plot of land. You cannot help noting that most of the inhabitants use both back and front garden for vegetables. Perhaps flower gardening is a luxury, and not to be afforded as yet; but it must also be remembered that the cultivation of flowers was not an African occupation.

But ugly or not, Orlando was a great municipal achievement, and a great boon to tens of thousands of people, who were living under conditions of great congestion and hardship. The African people from the farms and reserves have migrated in greater and greater numbers to Johannesburg, and Johannesburg has found work for many of them in her growing factories. But the pressure on African housing became unendurable. Sometimes people lived ten, fifteen, twenty in a two-roomed house.

Eventually even Orlando spilt over, and then came the shanty towns. These towns were built on the open veld, out of poles, sacks, boxes, and pieces of tin. They were built in desperation, and in defiance of the law. The largest of these shanty towns is Moroka, not far from Orlando, which contains over sixty thousand souls.

You will see that the conditions of these towns are very shocking; it is terrible that human beings should have to live under them. Yet, nevertheless, the total impression is not one of unrelieved filth and squalor. There are signs here, as there were in the house we visited at Western Native Township, of a great vitality, a will to make something out of nothing. This house here, that a strong wind would blow away, is a barber's shop, and if you look inside it, you will see that although it has the most primitive equipment, it is kept very clean. The plots of land on which these brave houses are built are uniformly twenty feet by twenty feet. And here of course are no gardens at all. It is supposed to be housing of the most temporary kind, but temporary housing in Johannesburg has a habit of going on forever.

Is this terrible housing shortage completely forgivable and understandable? It is not. These people who live here, played their part, too, in the building of the great city of Johannesburg. Expanding industry has given most of them a livelihood, but industry expanded only because it could get their labor. That there is a housing shortage one readily understands, that it persists with so little done one cannot forgive. Any decent white South African who visits the shanty towns must come away from them humble and ashamed.

In the years 1949, 1950, and 1951, the proud city of Johannesburg built not a single house for its African people, who, because they lived on municipal land, could not build houses for themselves. There were reasons, of course, for this failure to build; but the main reason was that reasons were put before people.

On our way back to Johannesburg we pass the big Non-European Hospital at Baragwanath. This was a British military hospital during the Second World War, and is now one of the finest non-European hospitals in the country. Even though much remains to be done, South Africa can be proud of the efforts she has made to bring medical and health services to her poorer peoples, and of the work that is being done for them by our doctors and nurses. In a country so ironbound by racial custom, many white men and women find an outlet for their altruistic impulses in the medical and nursing professions; and many others look at them wistfully, and envy them.

We will take an indirect route to Johannesburg so that we can see some of the suburbs in which the white people of Johannesburg live. As you will see, some of them are very beautiful, and speak of comfort and riches. I need not tell you that great inequality of wealth is dangerous to any society; but it is still more dangerous when opportunity is withheld by law.

And now we shall return by way of the University of Johannesburg, the largest in South Africa, with nearly five thousand students. It has a fine Medical School, and up till now has always admitted a certain number of nonwhite students. But the Government does not approve of this, and will no doubt take steps to bring it to an end, especially now that a fine nonwhite Medical School is being established at Durban, as part of the University of Natal.

By the way, in 1952 a tornado destroyed thousands and thousands of these shanty homes at a place called Albertynsville, not far from Moroka. The response of white people to this loss and suffering was immediate and warm; food and clothing were taken by motorists from all over the Witwatersrand. More than enough money was subscribed in a few days to replace all that was lost, and there was an outcry when the fund was closed on that account. Many white people had never seen such places before, and did not know how terrible some of them were.

I conclude with this so that you can get as complete a picture as possible of the situation as it is. But you would be quite right if you concluded that it often needs tornadoes to make things move.

11. A JOURNEY TO A MAGIC COUNTRY

Today we are going to travel nearly four hundred miles by automobile through new country. Get out your maps of the Transvaal and let us see where we are going. First we go to Pretoria, but we shall pretend not to see it, because we are going to spend a day there when we return. Then we go via Warmbad, Nylstroom, Naboomspruit, Potgietersrust, and Pietersburg to Louis Trichardt. Then we turn east and make for the great Park, entering by the gate called Punda Maria.

The early morning is cold in Johannesburg, but wear your light clothes, because not only shall we be in the tropics this afternoon, but we are going to lose more than four thousand feet of altitude, and the temperature is going to rise at least thirty degrees Fahrenheit.

North of Pretoria we are soon in what is known as the bushveld, a flat country covered with thorn forest. It is not what you would call a beautiful country, but it has a great fascination for South Africans, especially those who are fond of hunting, camping, and the open-air life. Already, if one has eyes for it, one can see that bird life is more plentiful and more striking in color than in the higher and colder regions.

The road over which we are traveling is called the Great North Road, and goes via Southern Rhodesia to the Victoria Falls (1,000 miles), through Northern Rhodesia to Nairobi in Kenya (2,000 miles), where it turns west to the Congo and to Nigeria (2,500 miles), finally turning north again for its last dangerous two thousand miles over the Sahara to Algiers. And we feel, too, that we are going north, nearer to the heart of the great continent of Africa. There is a feeling of excitement in the party; diamonds and gold are exciting enough, but

61

we are going to see one of the wonders of the creation.

This excitement is heightened when we reach Louis Trichardt, and study the many signposts in the middle of this small town under the mountains. There it is, plainly showing the road to the east, KRUGER NATIONAL PARK.

We have some food at one of the tearooms or *koffiekamers*. It is full of people, all talking. Some are going, some are coming back, but they all talk of the same things. If you listen you can hear what they are—lions, elephants, giraffes.

This eastern country through which we are now passing is a reserve for the Bavenda people, and much of it is relatively untouched by Western civilization. Many of these people we shall see, some in their tribal costumes, reminding us of the pictures that we saw in the Duggan-Cronin Gallery.

The Kruger National Park was founded by the late President Kruger, of the Transvaal Republic, in 1898. But soon after that came the Anglo-Boer War, and the Transvaal became a British Colony in 1902. Fortunately the Park project was proceeded with, and today it comprises a tract of country some two hundred miles long, and some thirty to sixty miles wide. Its area is eight thousand square miles, which is about the same as that of Massachusetts.

But look—there is a notice announcing that we are now entering the Park. There are few rules, but they are very strict. Here are most of them.

Keep to the traveling hours laid down.
Keep to the roads.
Keep inside your car.
Never leave a Camp except by vehicle (no open vehicle allowed).
Be in Camp by the specified time, usually sunset.
Never travel more than 25 m.p.h.
You may seek permission to take a firearm, but it may only be used
   in self-protection.

This last rule is no doubt for the very nervous; the great majority of visitors take no such thing.

Stop! Stop! Stop! What are those ahead of us? Lions, in our first half hour in the Park! Will they walk right up to us? Look, one of our party is taking no risks, she is winding up the window already. But all of us are strung up, full of excitement and anticipation, and a small dash of fear. But the two animals do not come up to us; they stop and look at us for a moment, as if uncertain. And they are not lions at all, they are wild dogs, and are fierce and savage hunters, preying on the smaller kinds of game. Then, while we sit transfixed, they turn off into the long grass, and are soon lost to view. We certainly were excited, but lions are seldom seen in this northern part of the Park.

And here is another notice, which says Beware of Elephants. You are warned in the Park literature to observe elephants from a distance, the only animals about which such a warning is given. If they obstruct your passage, you must return and find some other route, of which there are many in the Park. And there they are, a lordly herd of lordly animals, some thirty in number. We stop and watch them, for they are not likely to come in this direction. Bulls, cows, and calves, see how they destroy and uproot the trees! You will frequently come across their trails, wide swathes of destruction running through the bush, and great piles of dung left in the roads.

But the sun is sinking, and it is time we were in Camp. There it is, Punda Maria, our first camp, behind its stockade. There are sounds of talking and laughter, and some people are already grilling their meat over open fires. We pay our dues, and are given our rooms. The accommodation in the Park is simple but adequate. There are no hotels; some people would like them, but so far the authorities have resisted such demands. They want to keep the Park as natural as possible.

Darkness falls, and we, too, prepare our evening meal over the fires. We are truly in wild Africa at last. A fine mist falls, a strange phenomenon in this dry season. Outside the stockade is the African bush; this is the time when hunting begins, and you can hear the strange calls and cries of the veld. Death is stalking its prey, for it is the fiercest of all laws that prevails out there.

Yet for all that you yourself will feel excited and happy. All the problems of the world, of the United States, of South Africa and Johannesburg, are forgotten. Outside there is struggle and fear enough, but here inside is a strange feeling of peace and content. A number of people are gathered round a fire, singing popular Afrikaanse *liedjies:* "Sarie Marais," "Jan Pierewit," "Die Donkie is 'n wonderlike ding" (the donkey is a wonderful thing). One of them hears your American accents, and comes to ask you what you think of South Africa's Park; and if you speak of your own enjoyment and excitement, he will be pleased and proud.

And so to bed. But not always to sleep. Perhaps your excitement is too great. Perhaps some particularly fierce roar, some particularly loud cry of distress, awakens you, and you wonder what is happening out there. And most wonderful of all, your trip has hardly begun.

12. ELEPHANTS AND CROCODILES

Long before dawn the whole Camp is astir. Automobiles are being started up, and some are already standing at the gate, waiting for it to be opened. That is because the early hours of the day, and the hour before sunset, are the best times for seeing game.

Before we start on our journey south, we are going north to the boundary of the Park to see the hippos at Pafuri. Then we shall make for the south, passing through or staying at camps with wonderful names, Shingwidzi, Letaba, Satara, Nwanetzi, Skukuza, Pretoriuskop, Crocodile Bridge, and Malelane.

The University of Cape Town

Groote Schuur, the Great Barn, the residence
of the Prime Minister in Cape Town

Windermere, a suburb of Cape Town. In
the background is Table Mountain.
Photograph by Dan Weiner

The old Cape Malay quarter
of Cape Town

A main thoroughfare
in Kimberley

Victoria Falls is in Rhodesia, but easily
reached by plane from Johannesburg
Photograph from Three Lions

Johannesburg

Yellow mine dumps form the foreground to central Johannesburg

A native woman makes snuff in one of the outskirts
of Johannesburg
Photograph by Dan Weiner

Natives in the streets of Johannesburg. They are being brought to the gold mine compounds.
Photograph by Dan Weiner

Miners queue up for dinner at a gold mine
near Johannesburg
Photograph by Dan Weiner

The Voortrekker Monument at Pretoria is
opened by the Prime Minister

Sculptured wagons surround the base of Monument

A Boer farmer instructs his native workers

Photograph by Dan Weiner

A giraffe, elephant
and lions in Kruger
National Park

The Indian Quarter in Durban

An Indian woman returning from market
Photograph by Dan Weiner

Durban Bay and the Victoria Embankment

An African guide, probably a Shangaan, takes us to see the hippos. At first they are difficult to see if they are lying quietly in the water. Hardly anything is visible except the crown of the great flat head. Then the hippo submerges, and comes up again at some other place, enabling us to see more of him.

The Park is full of birds. Most notable and frequently seen are the lilac-breasted roller, the hornbills, the gray lourie, the wood shrike and the long-tailed shrike, the various glossy starlings, and flocks of Arnott's chats. The bateleur, one of the most magnificently colored of all the birds of prey, sails majestically overhead, sometimes uttering a deep cry, sometimes clapping its wings.

Over yonder is a great gathering of birds in the sky. From all directions they are joined by others. They are vultures, going to a kill. Soon they will alight, and wait for the killer to depart. Their heads are bald, and whether because of this or because they are always associated with death, they appear to us repulsive. But their work is useful; they are the scavengers of the wilds, and will pick the carcass clean of any scrap of flesh.

The greatest bird we shall see is of course the ostrich. It stands eight feet high, and is often seen in small parties. Ostriches have a powerful kick, and are fast runners, reaching a speed of thirty miles an hour, but they do not fly.

Those striking trees with the bright green trunks and branches are fever trees. Their presence is supposed to indicate that this is fever country, as indeed most of the Park is. That is why all this portion of the Park is closed in summer; but it is also because of the summer rains, which flood the *vleis* or marshes, and the dry river courses, and make the earth roads unusable. But there are perennial rivers too, rich in reeds and tall grass, and big spreading trees not seen in the drier parts of the Park. These rivers are the home of hippos and crocodiles, the playing grounds of the elephants, and the drinking places of thousands upon thousands of game of every kind.

Here is a place where we may leave the car, and a guide will take us down to the river to see the crocodiles. Again we feel excitement and anticipation, mixed with a dash of fear. But we are soon at ease, for our guide seems quite unperturbed; we note, however, that he carries a knobkerrie, which is a short stick with a large round head; also he carries a spear called an assegai.

He takes us to a little stockade, and we stand behind it so that we may watch the crocodiles unperceived. At first we cannot see them at all, but he shows us what looks like a log of wood on a little spit of sand in the river. Yes, it is a crocodile right enough, a dangerous and ugly creature for which man feels no affection. It lies motionless, covered in armor, with sleepy-looking but knowing eyes. Our guide makes a movement, and it slides off the spit in a flash, and with a loud splash it is gone.

We are now traveling south, toward Shingwidzi and Letaba. As we cross each vlei and watercourse, we look to left and to right with hope and anticipation. And there in a glade is one of the most beautiful sights of nature, a herd of impala, small antelopes which moving or at rest are graceful beyond description. We shall see them throughout the Park, and never tire of doing so.

And there, too, is one of the most comical sights of nature, a warthog on the run. He sticks his tail up like a ramrod pointing straight to heaven. Baboons will also be seen, searching for scorpions under the stones, carrying and scolding and de-fleaing their young.

I have told you that the Park is on the whole a flat country. But now and again one comes across an open point of vantage. Such sights are not easily forgotten. Mile after mile is stretched out before one a dense black sea of bush, with blue mountains on the horizon; it could be no other place than Africa.

The leading car has come to a stop, and is signaling to us to do likewise. They point frantically, but as happens so often here, there is absolutely nothing to be seen. Then suddenly one does see it; it was there all the time, lost in its own background of tree and grass and shadow. It is a kudu bull, proud and magnificent; how such a creature could be overlooked is a mystery. He stands and looks at the stationary cars; he is on the alert, but shows no sign of fear. His two great horns are deadly weapons, and even the lion will think twice before attacking him.

This tremendous tree that we see, with a gigantic trunk that suddenly stops dead and breaks into branches, is the *baobab* or the cream of tartar tree. And the bush through which we are now passing is called *mopani,* and covers thousands of square miles of this part of Africa. Look! Zebras and wildebeests, great numbers of each! They can be seen separately but for some reason they are usually found together.

And look, in that glade! Another of the most beautiful sights of the wilds, the fastest of all terrestrial creatures, the cheetahs, three of them. They are intent on some business, for they take no notice of us, and soon are lost in the depths and shadows of the sunset bush.

But we must not linger any more. It is drawing near to sunset, and we must be at Letaba before the gate closes. And round about Letaba, perhaps even from behind the stockade, we shall see more elephants, for this spot on the Letaba River is one of their drinking places.

Here is the Camp, with a character all its own, and as much part of these wilds as a man-made thing could be. Again we grill our meat over the fires, and recount the experiences of the day, trying to hide our disappointment that we have not yet seen a lion. But hardly have we fallen asleep than we are wakened by the only sound of its kind on the earth, the roaring of the king of beasts; now there is hope for tomorrow.

13. THE KING OF BEASTS

Before dawn we are ready, and when the gates open we are the first to pass through. The whole animal kingdom is active, and perhaps we shall be lucky enough to see lions before they retire for the day. But fortunately for us, according to the chief architect of this great Game Reserve, Colonel Stevenson-Hamilton, it is not the true habit of lions to retire for the day. Their true habit is diurnal, and more and more they are returning to it; they departed from it only because man the hunter was abroad, and this luckily is no longer the case, for here man hunts only with the camera.

You may reflect for a moment, if you wish to, on this great change in human behavior; for the most shocking stories are told of the wanton destruction of wild animals at the beginning of this century, often for no other purpose it would seem than for the pleasure of causing a living thing to die. Consider how human behavior has changed just because of the determination and persistence of a few humans who hated destruction, and who worked to conserve these treasures for the delight of the world. Let us have hope for the future, that other things may change also, which at this time seem rooted in human behavior. And that delicate creature standing there, so small and perfect, so utterly beautiful, is the steenbuck, one of the smallest of all antelopes. There is perfection already attained!

And that small animal there with the beautiful coat, watching us with such lively curiosity, is the jackal of a thousand legends and stories. We throw him an apple, which seems poor fare compared with the cruel delicacies of the bush. But he does not scorn it; perhaps he fared badly in the night, or perhaps he has a taste for fruit after meat, for he eats it to the end, then disappears into the bush.

And while it is still in my mind, let me tell you that Colonel Stevenson-Hamilton wrote a book called *A South African Eden,* which is all about the Park; and though it is true that the Colonel on the whole preferred the animals to the visitors, his book, like the Park, is so full of fascination that we easily forgive him.

There is a waterbuck; he, too, is an impressive animal, though he seems to lack the sublime self-containment of the lordly kudu. He stands by a skeleton, which looks as though it has been newly picked clean by the vultures. Why he stands there, and what it has to do with him, we cannot inquire. But these skeletons are to be seen throughout the Park, and are reminders of the law by which the bush lives. Yet, according to the Colonel, the bush is not a place of terror. And I myself have seen, after wild dogs had pulled down and were tearing to pieces a wildebeest calf, that the whole herd passed immediately from panic to quiet, and moved away a short distance to continue their feeding, except for the restless and frantic mother, who nevertheless herself calmed down and rejoined the others when it was clear that the short, swift drama was over. It seems that animals know when they are menaced and when they are not, that they know when the hunter is hunting and when he is not, and that they do not fear when there is nothing to fear. It is a strange world; we do not understand it, and it is worth listening only to the views of one who long and faithfully observed it, especially when he can express them in language such as this:

"Except in carefully guarded sanctuaries it is difficult to study wild creatures fully. Elsewhere, on Man's presence being detected, all the little intimacies of animal life stop dead. His tyranny is to himself so much a matter of course, that, especially if he is of the great majority who live their lives divorced from wild nature, he views the frenzied terror which the creatures display on his approach, as being their natural habit of life. From a place of concealment, you are looking over an African river scene. Tree-clad banks and green reeds fringe the water, which reflects the pure blue of the sky. Hippos splash and grunt, crocodiles float lazily about among unheeding fishes; otters protrude their heads, turn over in the water like seals, or lie lazily on stones by its edge; a pair of Egyptian geese are preening themselves on a sandbank; kingfishers poise and dive; bush pheasants strut about, and call raucously to one another; a bateleur sails overhead; two fish eagles perch side by side on a dead bough; a long line of impala makes its slow way towards the water, stealthily watched by a leopard extended along the horizontal limb of a great fig tree.

"It is hard to realize that so peaceful a scene is all a part of the great process of eating and being eaten. And then, the moment you show yourself, what a change! The hippos and the crocodiles dive; the others disappear in water or burrow; the birds fly away; the impala snort and rush off; the leopard has simply vanished. In a few seconds not a sign of animal life is left visible to the human eye. Unvarying reaction to the recognition of wild nature's arch enemy." *

And here again we come to one of the rare points of vantage in the Park, a high rocky point. To the north is the black endless sea of bush, where lie Letaba, Shingwidzi, and Punda Maria, from which we have come; to the south is the endless sea of bush also, but in the far distance can be seen the peaks of Pretoriuskop, towards which we are going; to the east is the endless sea of bush and the vast country of Mozambique; to the west the same, but there is the escarpment of the Drakensberg, the Mountains of the Dragon, and beyond that the interior plateau of Southern Africa. And look, on the rock high above us, beautiful and motionless, silhouetted against the sky, the *klipspringer*, the rock jumper, another antelope, of its kind perfection. He is quite still, and appears to be surveying the world as still as he below him. But someone waves a handkerchief to him, and suddenly where he was there is nothing to be seen at all.

The road descends from the rocky height, and soon we are in a flat stretch of country, dotted with larger acacias, and clean of undergrowth and smaller vegetation. And there must be something there, for all the cars have stopped, and the people in them seem very excited. For a moment we see nothing, and then suddenly the hidden picture is seen. A giraffe, by all that's wonderful! There it is, the

* From *A South African Eden*, by Colonel Stevenson-Hamilton, published by Cassell & Company Ltd. Used by permission.

fabulous creature, with the fabulous neck and legs. It looks at us over the top of one of the trees, and the tree itself is at least sixteen feet in height. What a wonderful creature, or rather what wonderful creatures, for now we can see two, three . . . at least nine of them. They stop eating and stand motionless and observe us; then they decide that too many of us are gathering, and begin to move away quietly as though they hoped not to be observed, but one of the cars starts off, and they break into a strange ungainly canter. We did not see much of them, but we shall see many more before we leave. By the way, the Afrikaans word for giraffe is *kameelperd,* which is close to an old English word camelopard, now never used in ordinary conversation, but meaning camel-horse. But for some reason it is the word giraffe, of Arabian extraction, that has finally won the day.

I have told you that the Park is a dry region, but now we come to a miniature lake, rich in water lilies of a lovely light blue color. The lake is fringed with reeds, and is set like a jewel in this harsh dry world. And there on its edge stands the tall marabou stork, with a beak twice as long as its head, colored vividly in red and yellow and black. He does not like the look of us, and spreads his great wings to fly across the water lilies; you will not see such a scene again in the Kruger Park, yet strangely you will not see it anywhere else, except in some similar part of Africa.

We travel on slowly, and let us admit it, by this time our eyes are searching the bush desperately for some sign of the king of beasts. How disappointing to go back home and admit we did not see him! But it so turns out that we have searched the bush in vain, for suddenly before us, lying placidly and contentedly in the very road, not wild dogs this time, but lions, one, two, three, four, five, and three lion cubs. They must have just come here, for there are no cars here but our own. They take no notice of us at all, but they have been known to cluster round a car, to rear up and put their paws on the radiator, even to look in at a window. One is supposed to keep quiet and self-possessed under such circumstances, and to do nothing at all. There is no record of any attack by a lion on passengers in a car, though elephants have been known to turn vehicles over; that is why tourists are asked to treat elephants with extra respect.

It was at one time supposed that the various smells of the automobile were so strong that the lions could not recognize the smell of man. Colonel Stevenson-Hamilton once thought so himself, but further observation led him to believe that they did in fact scent human beings, but having had no experience of hostile action so long as these human beings remained in their cars, they had no fear. The Colonel himself has on occasion started to get out of the car, and the lions have jumped up ready to bolt, only to lie down again when he re-entered the car. He insists again and again that the lion is not an animal obsessed with the thought of killing men, that only under special circumstances does he turn man-eater, and that his general inclination is to give way to men; *but under no circumstances whatsoever must it be forgotten that the lion is a formidable beast of rapine.* Therefore obey the rules of the Park.

So now you see that all the photographs of lions lying in the roads were true. Many visitors to the Park have seen lions pulling down and tearing to pieces their prey, and other grim contests of the wilds, with the participants quite oblivious of the presence of human spectators.

We have still another day in the Park, and we may yet see eland, the greatest of the antelopes; the sable, rivaling the kudu in magnificence; and a number of other antelopes that we shall recognize only by careful study of the guidebook, inyala, roan, duiker, tsessebe, bushbuck, and reedbuck.

You will remember that we entered the Park via Louis Trichardt and Punda Maria; by this route the descent from the interior plateau was gradual and unspectacular. But we shall return via Bushbuckridge, Kowyn's Pass, and Pilgrim's Rest, over the escarpment known as the Drakensberg Mountains.

This part of the country is extremely beautiful; it is almost in the tropics, yet it is high and enjoys an abundant rainfall. Although we are here in the dry months of winter, it is clear that this is a well-favored region. Nothing could be in sharper contrast with the dry acacia savannah from which we have just come.

We proceed via Lydenburg to Machadodorp and Middelburg. This is all grass country, though much more attractive than the drier Western Transvaal. We pass through Witbank, which is clearly a coal-mining district; but as we approach Springs we see again the familiar white dumps of the gold mines of the Reef, and for the last hour's journey to Johannesburg they are the most striking features of the landscape.

We are back in civilization, having seen such sights as are not seen by many, and are refreshed and fortified to study further the habits, peculiarities, and achievements of the human race.

14. PRETORIA

Pretoria, as you know, is the administrative capital of the Union of South Africa, and Cape Town is the legislative capital. This was one of the compromises that made the Union of the four provinces possible. It means that thousands of public servants must leave Pretoria each January and travel to Cape Town for the Parliamentary Session, which usually lasts until May. In actual fact everyone thinks of Pretoria as the capital of South Africa, and you will hear very often that Pretoria has decided so-and-so, but you will seldom hear Cape Town spoken of in the same way.

Pretoria is much more an Afrikaans-speaking city than either Cape Town or Johannesburg. This is partly a matter of history, because Pretoria was the capital city of the old Transvaal Republic; and it is partly because Pretoria is the home of the Public Service, which is overwhelmingly staffed by Afrikaners. Four other services are also overwhelmingly staffed by Afrikaners; one is the South African Police, *die Suid-afrikaanse Polisie,* the second is the South African Railways, *die Suid-afrikaanse Spoorweë,* the third is the Postal Service, *die Poswese,* the fourth is the Union Defense Force, *die Unie-verdedigingsmag.* On the contrary you will find that commerce and industry are largely in English-speaking hands. Farmers are also predominantly Afrikaans-speaking, except in Natal, where they are predominantly English-speaking. The gold industry, the diamond industry, the entertainment industry, the motor industry, all are largely controlled by English-speaking people; but for some reason which I cannot give you, the undertaking profession, that is the profession of morticians, has largely passed into Afrikaner hands.

The two great commercial banks of the country are Barclays and the Standard, both with head offices in London. Although these banks now do business in both languages, yet the Afrikaner Nationalist was dissatisfied to be served by a "foreign" bank, and so established the Volkskas, which is growing in importance. I would guess that its personnel is one hundred per cent Afrikaans-speaking.

Pretoria has the most striking city square in South Africa, namely Church Square. It is flanked by many fine buildings, one of which is the *Raadzaal,* that is, the Council Hall, which was the home of the Volksraad of the old Transvaal Republic. Flying from it are two flags, one the Union Jack, the other the Union Flag. This again is a compromise of which we shall learn more, but this is one of the few places outside Natal where the Union Jack, the flag of Britain, still flies.

It flies also from the principal government buildings in the capitals of the Union, and at Union ports, while in Natal it flies from Magistrates' Courts and other government buildings in the more English-speaking centers of the province.

On the Union Flag itself you will notice three small flags in the center. These are the Union Jack, and the two flags of the old Republics, the Transvaal and the Orange Free State. This is another compromise.

If you went to some official public function, you would hear two national anthems; one is "God Save the Queen," and the other is *"Die Stem van Suid-afrika."* This is also a compromise. If you went to some big Afrikaner function, you would certainly not hear both anthems; but if you went to some big English-speaking function, the chances are that you would.

In Church Square is the statue of President Kruger. He was President of the Transvaal Republic in 1886 when gold was discovered on the Witwatersrand; and it was he who saw the independence of the republic threatened by the inrush of gold-seeking strangers, and who fiercely resisted the plans of Cecil John Rhodes and Lord Milner. Apart from the Voortrekker heroes of whom we shall soon learn, President Paul Kruger is the supreme figure of Afrikaner history, and typifies for Afrikaners the courage and sturdiness of their race. He wore a frock coat and a top hat, and was bearded and patriarchal, a faithful reader of the Bible, and a lover of the pipe.

We shall visit the house where the President lived, which is now a museum. His last days were not happy; in 1899 began the Anglo-Boer War, called by the Afrikaners *die Vryheidsoorlog,* or the War of Freedom. The President went to Switzerland and died there old and in exile in 1904, two years after Britain had won the war. He sent a last message to his people: *Take the best from the past and build your future on it.*

Although his end was tragic, his life and work were not. Today, fifty years after the war, not the Transvaal alone, but all South Africa, is ruled by an Afrikaner Prime Minister and an Afrikaner Cabinet. It is true that South Africa is not a Republic, but a member of the British Commonwealth of Nations; however, no external compulsion keeps her so.

Kruger was for seventeen years the President and father of his people. He would give them audience on the *stoep* of his house, one of his favorite times being six o'clock in the morning. He was a strong and vivid personality, and many stories are told of him.

Pretoria is the fourth city of the Union of South Africa; Johannesburg, Cape Town, and Durban are the first three. The population of Pretoria is approaching 300,000.

If the handiwork of man is to be considered, as it should be in the making of a city, then Pretoria is the most beautiful of South African cities. The people of Pretoria are true gardeners, and even now in this winter month of June can be seen traces of their wonderful rose gardens. These trees that we see lining so many streets are the jacarandas; they flower in October and November, and in cool dull weather the blue blossoms drop and lie unfaded on the ground, giving to the streets a fantastic beauty.

Pretoria, being the administrative capital, contains many fine buildings. The finest group of these is to be seen round Church Square, the central space contributing much to their beauty. But there is one building in Pretoria which will always stand alone, and that is the Union Buildings,* the administrative home of government. These buildings are magnificently sited, being built below the summit of Meintjeskop. The buildings themselves are magnificent; they consist of two great wings, meeting in a semicircular amphitheater, commanded by two domed towers. The architect was that same Herbert Baker who built Groote Schuur for Cecil Rhodes.

The Union Buildings are surrounded by beautiful gardens, and from them is to be had a magnificent view of Pretoria. Look, there is Church Square, and there are the buildings of the University of Pretoria, which teaches in the Afrikaans language, just as the University of the Witwatersrand, in Johannesburg, teaches in English. That prominent structure on the ridge yonder is the Voortrekker Monument, and we shall now set out to visit it, stopping for a moment before we leave the Union Buildings to admire the statue of General Louis Botha, the first Prime Minister of the Union of South Africa.

* It is hard to know whether to use a singular or plural verb when speaking of the Union Buildings. Buildings is a plural noun, but the Union Buildings are (is?) one single building.

This is not, of course, the first time we have seen the Voortrekker Monument in the distance. We saw it on our trip to the Kruger National Park, and we saw it again this morning as we came from Johannesburg, and for a great part of the journey, too, for it occupies a dominating position.

This is the monument to the Voortrekkers, the pioneers, those Boers who left the colony of the Cape of Good Hope in the 1830's, and crossed the Orange River (as we have done), seeking a country of their own where they might live free from British rule. This Great Trek was made by ox-wagons, the prairie schooners of South Africa, and both the ox and the wagon play a great part in Afrikaner thought, poetry, and symbolism. It is not surprising therefore to see that this massive granite memorial is surrounded at its base by a wall of sculptured oxen and wagons, joined together in what is called in Nederlands a *laager*, in Afrikaans a *laer*. The *laager* or *laer* of ox-wagons was the defense of the trekkers against the African tribesmen who contested their passage; the whole company gathered inside it, the men firing through the open spaces, the women handing them the ammunition, or in times of stress, fresh-loaded weapons. Frequently the laager was strengthened by thorn trees, *doringbome*, a tree so much part of the land and of the trekkers' lives, that it, too, figures in Afrikaner thought as a symbol of toughness and endurance in a dry and jealous land. This wall of wagons has also a second symbolic purpose, and that is to ward off the entry of everything that clashes with Voortrekker tradition into this Afrikaner shrine.

The monument is a hundred and thirty feet high, but its material impressiveness lies in its massiveness, not its height. We pass up many steps, through the laager, and into the lower hall of the monument, in which is the cenotaph, the symbolic grave of Piet Retief and his men, who gave their lives for their people. Of this tragic event we shall soon be learning. On the cenotaph are inscribed the words: *Ons vir jou, Suid-Afrika,* which means We for Thee, South Africa.

These words are taken from the hymn which is now accepted as one of the two anthems of the Union of South Africa. On the sixteenth day of December each year the rays of the sun fall through an opening in the dome of the monument, and illumine these words. The sixteenth day of December is the date of the decisive battle of Blood River, about which you will also soon be learning.

Above the Lower Hall is the Hall of Heroes. This contains a magnificent frieze in Italian marble, depicting the history of the Great Trek in twenty-seven tableaux.

On the four outside corners of the monument are four huge granite figures, representing Piet Retief, Andries Pretorius, Hendrik Potgieter, and a fourth representative of the Voortrekkers in general.

In front of the monument stands Anton van Vouw's great statue of the Voortrekker woman as mother. This occupies the place of honor in recognition of the heroic part of the Voortrekker women in making possible the establishment of white civilization in South Africa.

The foundation stone of the monument was laid on December 16, 1938, and it was opened on December 16, 1949, when it is estimated that a quarter of a million people gathered together, one tenth of the white population of South Africa.

One last interesting fact must be mentioned. On Tuesdays the monument is closed to Europeans, and may on that day be visited by non-Europeans.

The monument was built to commemorate the struggle of Christianity against Barbarism, and that means, to put it bluntly, the struggle of the Voortrekkers against the African people. This struggle is portrayed in a restrained and dignified fashion, but the fact remains that this is first and last an Afrikaner shrine. This greatest monument in South Africa (which is now simply called The Monument) evokes no more than a formal respect from anyone who is not an Afrikaner. The symbolic laager of wagons, which was intended to shut out anything that is not Afrikaner, succeeds only too well in its excluding purpose.

Is there any one symbol, any one thing, in South Africa which calls forth a common feeling from all South Africans? There is certainly no monument, no hero, no patriotic song, no commemorated day, which does so. The nearest we come to it is when we sing together one of the inimitable Afrikaans folk songs, or praise together the natural beauties of our native land. And even then we are often able to invest a mountain with political emotion.

The story is told by Dr. Malherbe, Afrikaans-speaking Principal of the English-speaking University of Natal, of an Afrikaner teacher who taught English at an Afrikaner school, and began his lesson with the words, *"Kinders, laat ons nou met die vyand se taal worstel,"* which is, Children, let us now wrestle with the enemy's language.

Such a story as the one I have just told you, would be much less likely to cause offense today than twenty years ago; and that is partly because more and more English-speaking people can understand it in the Afrikaans version and see its humor. Let us remember that physical conflicts between English-speaking and Afrikaans-speaking South Africans, except on isolated occasions created by exceptional circumstances, have occurred seldom over the period of fifty years since the Anglo-Boer War.

Nevertheless, no one could say that the group relations are cordial. In fact, there are many white South Africans who maintain that group relations amongst all the many groups in the country will be best and soundest when such groups go their own separate ways, pursuing their own separate goals, but respecting one another's pride and integrity. It is an attractive doctrine, and we shall have to consider it later.

Whatever else you say about us, you must admit that ours is not a dull country.

15. THE COMING OF THE DUTCH

How did it come about that Afrikaans-speaking and English-speaking South Africans remained so separate? Why do Afrikaners so often speak bitterly about Britain? And so bitterly about Rhodes and Milner? Why do they react warily to questions about missionary work in South Africa?

Why are the English-speaking people so lukewarm about the Voortrekker Monument, sometimes even sarcastic? Why do English-speaking people often blame Afrikaners for repressive aspects of race legislation?

How did it come about that racial custom and law became so rigid, especially in relation to color? Was Afrikaner opinion more responsible for this than English opinion? Is it true that English opinion is more liberal than Afrikaner opinion, but that English practice is just the same?

And what do the Africans themselves think of the policies of racial separation? What is their own interpretation of South African history?

I do not really know if you feel able to answer these questions. I certainly do not wish to answer them for you. What I intend to do is to give you a brief account of South African history, and this will certainly throw a great deal of light on these questions, and will perhaps help you to answer some of them for yourselves.

But it is important that you should know something about the person who is acting as your guide through South African history. I am a white English-speaking South African, born in the largely English-speaking Province of Natal. In childhood I never heard any Afrikaans spoken, but learned at home to feel sympathy for the language and culture struggle of the Afrikaner people; and later learned to speak the language itself, studied its literature, and the history of its people.

All these attempts to appreciate and to understand were strengthened by religious motives. Later at University (at college as you would say) I learned to take an even wider view, and to understand and to sympathize with the aspirations of the African and Colored peoples, and of our three hundred thousand Indians in Natal. This direction once taken, I did not deviate from it, and am now not likely ever to do so.

Such a view, to use a word taken from the late General Smuts, is *holistic*. The tendency of the person holding such a view, is to widen the group to which he belongs until it virtually includes the whole human race. But this holistic view is far from being the dominant white view in South Africa, and is far from being the view of the Government. A person who holds this holistic view usually states good intellectual reasons for doing so, but will also be found to have strong emotional reasons, some of them religious, some even unconscious.

A person who holds this holistic view cannot really accept rigid theories of racial separation. He cannot accept a Parliament which is representative only of white people, or which allows only limited representation of nonwhite people. Naturally he could never accept "separate but not necessarily equal" facilities for the various races; but neither can he accept "separate but equal" because in the final resort (which is Parliament), the theory becomes impossible.

A person who holds a holistic view cannot therefore accept the racial principles of Afrikaner Nationalism. A holist cannot really be much of a Nationalist. All that a holist can hope to do is to present Afrikaner Nationalism fairly. This I shall try to do. However, I shall not try to conceal my own views from you, but I shall not try to force them upon you. This is a book to show you South Africa, not to tell you what you must believe about it; but it cannot help telling you what I believe about it. I am like a teacher, who enjoys hearing your ideas, who enjoys telling you his own, but has no plan to make you think as he does. If you think as he does, that may please him; but if you do not, the honesty of your thought will please him just as well. That is just the difference between *education* and *indoctrination*. And now let us make a start with that history.

Herodotus, the great historian of antiquity, tells how Necho, King of Egypt, sent ships down the east coast of Africa, and how in the third year they returned to Egypt via the Mediterranean. That was six hundred years before Christ, and doubtless these mariners must have seen the mountain masses of the Cape.

Two thousand years later, in A.D. 1486, Bartholomew Diaz is said to have discovered the Cape. As you know, he called it first the Cape of Storms, and then either he or King John of Portugal renamed it the Cape of Good Hope.

In 1497 another great navigator, Vasco de Gama, passed beyond the Cape to discover and name Natal, and to find a new route to India.

In 1503 Antonio de Saldanha entered Table Bay, and his ship was perhaps the first ever to lie under the great mountain. He was almost certainly the first white man to climb it, and he it was who gave it its name of Table Mountain.

In 1602 the Dutch East India Company was formed to trade between Holland and the Dutch East Indies. So many ships were now passing on this route that the Company in 1652 sent out Jan van Riebeeck to found a refreshment station at the Cape, where green vegetables could be grown as a means of fighting the dread disease of scurvy, where outgoing sailors could leave letters to be taken back to Holland by some other ship, and where the very sick could be left for attention.

The indigenous inhabitants of the Cape were not numerous. They were the Hottentots and the Bushmen. The Hottentots were a primitive pastoral people; some of them were drawn into the life of the new settlement, some of them retreated north and northeast into the interior. The Bushmen were an even more primitive people; they were diminutive in stature, they were great hunters with poisoned arrows, and they have left behind fascinating rock paintings in caves.

When they could not get meat, they lived on wild melons, insects, and roots. With the coming of European civilization, they withdrew farther and farther, into mountain fastnesses or into the desert. They raided the white men's cattle and possessions, and the white men in their turn pursued and killed them. Today there are few of them left; they live in the Kalahari Desert, and are protected by the Government, in much the same way as the wild animals of the Kruger Park.

The Dutch East India Company did not intend this new settlement to be a colony. Nevertheless it did not find company farming altogether successful, and in 1657 it allowed nine burghers to go farming on their own at Rondebosch, but placed them under many restrictions. In fact the burghers grew more and more impatient of the rule of the Dutch East India Company.

The Company offered such low prices for vegetables that in 1658, in an attempt to lower the costs of production, the first Negro slaves were imported from West Africa. Many of these ran away, ignorant of the thousands of miles that stretched between the Cape and their homes, much of it trackless and waterless. Then slaves from Malaya were imported to take their places. Is it not indeed fantastic to think that there was once such a traffic in human beings? In the Cape fortunately slavery took a mild form, and there do not survive in South Africa the terrible stories known in so many other countries. We can be thankful that slavery has been swept from the earth, but this advance must be maintained by the vigilance of all free men; for it is always a temptation to men with power to use other men as tools.

The Hottentots adapted themselves in part to the new order of things. Some became Christians, and Jan van Riebeeck allowed the marriage of Eva, a Hottentot girl who had been brought up in his household, to the surgeon van Meerhof. But as society became more settled, such marriages became less and less acceptable; the Hottentot people merged rather with the slaves from the East, and with an infusion of white blood from settlers and sailors there grew up in the Cape a separate people called the Cape Coloreds, who today are about a million in number, and speak the language called Afrikaans.

The white people of the Cape grew slowly in numbers, and were strengthened by small numbers of German and French immigrants, the latter of whom brought vines to the Colony. Many of them were townspeople, and stayed in Cape Town, but the more adventurous were attracted by the great mountains and fertile valleys of the Cape. They moved farther and farther away from the shadow of Table Mountain. The most adventurous became pastoralists rather than agriculturists, and trekked into the wastes of the Karroo with their flocks and herds. They were already impatient of the rule of the Company, and they lived in isolation from the influences of Europe. Their Dutch language changed in a fascinating way, becoming much simplified, and adding to itself a host of new idioms influenced by the kind of country they lived in and the kind of life they led, by the ox, by the wagon, by the loneliness, by the dry watercourse and the thorn. This country was as unlike Holland as any country could be, and the language had to find new names for it, and give new meanings to old words. The language was called simply *die taal* or the language, but is today called Afrikaans. The people were called the Afrikanders, the people of Africa; today they are Afrikaners.

The expansion over the Karroo was rapid. Smallpox had almost annihilated the Hottentots, and there was little to stop the advance of the trekker, or the *trekboer* as he was called, or even more simply, the Boer. The word boer means farmer; and the word trekboer means a farmer who treks about, looking for grazing. The Company tried to control this migration, but was not successful; and this hard but free life made the trekkers independent and impatient of control.

Such conditions of isolation and wildness might have led to degeneration, but religion exercised a powerful influence over the people. The Church, like the Company, found it difficult to keep in touch with the trekkers, but the Bible was their constant companion. In particular were they attracted by the stories of the patriarchs, which seemed most relevant to their hard and lonely life. And who could have been nearer to the patriarchs than they themselves, as they moved in the wilderness with their flocks and herds, with their menservants and their maidservants, amongst wild men and wild beasts, with no protection but their rifles and their God? As for the land itself, with its space and freedom, with its oases of greenness and coolness amid the heat and rock and thorn, to it they gave a fierce and possessive love. How far indeed were they from Europe, and how far in this Karroo from the thousand waterways of Holland! This horse, this saddle, this rifle, this antelope running, this everlasting plain, this everlasting sun—this was life, yet you would not find one hint of it in all the picture galleries of Amsterdam.

About 1770 there were over ten thousand white people at the Cape, of which nine tenths were burghers and not Company officials; and about an equal number of slaves. About half of these burghers lived in Cape Town and in the beautiful valleys near it. But the other half were the trekboers of whom we have already spoken.

It was just about this time that those trekkers who remained nearer the coasts encountered the Bantu tribes moving south, largely in the coastal country below the southern and eastern escarpments. This was one of the supreme events in the history of the Afrikaner. These enemies did not waste away like the Bushmen and the Hottentots. They were called the Xosas, they were fierce warriors of assegai and shield, they were masters of barbaric song and dance, and they had a notable and intricate system of law and custom. They were cattle lovers, and the meaning of cattle to them is so important that we must discuss it later. Needless to say, their interests conflicted sharply with those of the trekboer. Both had need of grazing for their beasts.

Where did the Xosas come from? It is supposed that they came with the Nguni from the region of Victoria Nyanza, leaving there in the 1300's. It is supposed that it was this same need of grazing for their cattle that brought them south. Experts, by limiting their search to those regions through which a cattle-owning people could pass, have claimed to trace their journey by finding in what places their language picked up new words or left its own behind. This seems a fruitful method of research, because the journey of the Nguni people lasted over two hundred years, and it is believed that the Xosas arrived in the eastern Cape Province in the late 1500's, and would have reached the Cape itself in due course, had they not now encountered the Boers.

Be that as it may, the Company entered into a treaty with some Xosa chiefs, and declared the Fish River to be the boundary between the Boers and the Bantu. This act was useless. Individuals crossed the river, either to steal cattle or to retrieve them, and soon all were involved. There was incessant trouble, raiding, thefts, reprisals, breaking out into war. Sometimes a farmer would return home from a journey to find that his whole family had been killed, his home burned, his animals stolen. Grim pictures of these events are still to be found on the walls of some Afrikaner homes, keeping alive memories of the days when white and black were bitter enemies.

In this situation the Company was of little use. It had made the Fish River the boundary, but could do little to defend it. What was worse, one of its chief officials in these parts was a man called Maynier, who was inclined to favor the Xosas in these frontier disputes. The whole border was in a state of chaos, and less and less did the trekboers look for salvation anywhere but in themselves.

So it was that the struggle to survive on a dangerous continent became the main thought of the trekboer's mind, the main purpose of the trekboer's life. Like the thorn tree, he put his roots down into the rock and stone, and in the face of all calamity survived. His enmity with the black man was bitter and relentless, as was the black man's enmity with him. Between white men and black men, and more still between white men and black women, there could be no relationship except those of master and servant, or enemy and enemy. The Boer could only survive by keeping himself apart; only in *apartheid* was there any hope for the future of himself, his children, and his race.

And now, in the early 1800's, the British annexed the Cape, and inherited its turbulent frontier troubles.* The Dutch East India Company had become insolvent in 1798, and the days of Holland as a great power were over. At this time there were about 25,000 Europeans in the Colony, and rather more than that number of slaves.

So began the turbulent nineteenth century, which General Smuts was to call the Century of Wrong.

16. THE COMING OF THE BRITISH

With the coming of the British officials to the Cape, there came also a number of vigorous missionaries. The white farmers were used to officials, but the missionaries were something new. As might be expected, the attitude of the missionaries to the Hottentots and the Xosas was not the same as that of the farmers; to the missionaries they were souls to be saved, to the farmer they were laborers in whose educational and social advance he was not much interested, though he sometimes took an interest in their spiritual welfare. So officials, missionaries, and farmers lived in an uneasy triangular relationship. The officials had to consider the difficulties of the farmers, but they had also to consider the powerful support in England for the missionaries. These missionaries sent back reports to England, many of them hostile to the colonists.

Equally were the colonists hostile to the missionaries. Hottentots flocked to the mission stations, where they found conditions easier than on the farms. The farmers were angry at losing their labor, and regarded the religious zeal of the Hottentots as so much pretense, which no doubt it sometimes was. They were angered also by the missionary Vanderkemp, who himself no longer young, married a young Hottentot girl whose sole possessions were two sheepskins and some beads.

* The British actually occupied the Cape twice, first from 1795-1803, and again in 1806.

Things had changed since Eva married the surgeon van Meerhof with the approval of the Commander. By his marriage this newcomer Vanderkemp had affronted Afrikaner opinion; and in any case the white farmer could not see the point of educating nonwhites for a life that simply did not exist.

In 1815, under a new law, a Hottentot servant complained of the treatment he had received from his master, Frederick Bezuidenhout. Bezuidenhout treated the summons of the court with contempt, and at last a European officer with Hottentot soldiers was sent to arrest him. To send Hottentots to arrest a white man had never been done before. Bezuidenhout fought the party from a cave, but was killed. At his funeral his brother swore to avenge the outrage, and he and his friends rebelled. The rebellion was soon put down, and five of the men were hanged as rebels at Slagter's Nek; but by many of the farmers they were regarded as martyrs who had died for the cause of the white man against the Government, the missionaries, and the cursed doctrines of equality. Slagter's Nek is to this day remembered, one of the great and bitter events of the Century of Wrong.

In 1820 came the first large group of English-speaking colonists, about five thousand in number. Most of the settlers came to the disturbed frontier area, and they founded the town of Port Elizabeth. One result of their coming was to make the British Government attempt to anglicize the Afrikaner Dutch, and English took the place of Dutch as the official language. The Dutch *landdrosts* were replaced by magistrates, the Dutch *rix-dollars* by pounds, shillings, and pence, and only English and Latin were taught in the state-aided schools. This attempt at anglicization angered the Afrikaner Dutch, and even today the name of the Governor, Lord Charles Somerset, is remembered with detestation.

In 1828 missionary influence brought about the passage of the Fiftieth Ordinance, which secured the civil rights of colored people. This evidence of a further move towards equality also angered the farmers.

They saw the weakening of authority over the Hottentots, who could hardly be described as an industrious people; they feared increased vagrancy, greater idleness, and shortages of labor.

In 1834 the slaves of the Colony were emancipated. For slaves worth £3,000,000, compensation of £1,250,000 was to be paid, unfortunately in London. And in accordance with the Fiftieth Ordinance, these liberated slaves might go where they pleased.

Finally in 1834 there was the Sixth Kaffir War. The Xosas came across the frontier, burning, destroying, killing. They were driven back, and the Governor, Sir Benjamin D'Urban, fixed a new frontier on the Kei River. But the British Government reversed his policy, brought the frontier back to the Fish River, and declared that "the Kaffirs had an ample justification" for the war.

That was enough. The farmers had had enough. Of British Government, British missionaries, British public opinion, they had had enough. So five thousand of them set out north on the Great Trek, leaving the eastern coasts, climbing the mountains on to the great interior plain, in the direction of Kimberley and Bloemfontein and Johannesburg, all yet unborn; among the trekkers was a lad of ten, whose name was Paul Kruger. The year of the Great Trek is usually set down as 1836. "We quit this Colony," wrote Pieter Retief, one of the foremost Voortrekkers, "under the full assurance that the English Government has nothing more to require of us, and will allow us to govern ourselves without its interference in future."

A Voortrekker woman, Anna Steenkamp, wrote ". . . the shameful and unjust proceedings with reference to the freeing of our slaves; and yet it is not so much their freeing which drove us to such lengths, as their being placed on an equal footing with Christians, contrary to the laws of God, and the natural distinctions of race and color, so that it was intolerable for any decent Christian to bow down beneath such a yoke; wherefore we rather withdrew in order to preserve our doctrines in purity." There seems to be no doubt that one of the deepest causes of the Great Trek was the implication in British law and administration that white and nonwhite were in some way equal.

After much hardship and danger, the Voortrekkers finally broke the Bantu power in the interior plain, and settled in what today are called the Orange Free State and the Transvaal. Retief himself went down the escarpment of the Drakensberg into Natal, where a terrible calamity overtook him. With sixty followers he went to see the Zulu King Dingaan to make a treaty, but he and his whole party were murdered. The King then sent ten thousand warriors to the Voortrekker camp, where a few men had stayed behind to guard the women and children, and slaughtered them all, at *Weenen,* which name means weeping. Fortunately a new leader was ready to lead the Voortrekkers, Andries Pretorius, after whom Pretoria was named. On December 16, 1838, after having vowed to God to keep the day holy if He would give them victory, Pretorius humbled Dingaan's armies at the Battle of Blood River.

Thus December 16 was called Dingaan's Day for more than a century, and only recently has its name been changed to the Day of the Covenant. It is religiously observed by many Afrikaners, but not by English-speaking South Africans, who, until prevented by a growing uneasiness, and finally by law, used it to hold race-meetings and cricket matches. It is fair to say that the Day of the Covenant means little to the English-speaking South African; while to the African, the black man, it gives offense. And indeed this is not surprising, for the Day is often used by Afrikaner speakers to dwell on the bitter enmities of the past, and the necessity for continuing them into the future. Nothing could show more clearly than the Day of the Covenant, the terrible divisions of South Africa.

The Voortrekkers finally established the Republic of Natal in 1838, but it was short-lived. British traders and missionaries had been active at Durban Bay and along the Natal Coast since the year 1824, and had actually obtained a grant of land from the Zulu tyrant Tshaka before he was murdered by Dingaan. (In 1835 missionaries arrived from the United States also.) However, the British Government did not recognize the existence of this British settlement until the Boer Republic in 1841, sent a punitive expedition to the south against the Bacas, who had stolen some cattle. The neighboring Pondos were alarmed and appealed to the Cape Government, whereupon the British annexed Natal. The Dutch besieged the British in Durban, and Dick King, a British settler, made his famous ride of six hundred miles to Grahamstown in ten days, through a country wild and unknown, to call for reinforcements. Most of the Voortrekkers then trekked back over the escarpment, and Natal, as a result of immigration from Britain, became the largely English-speaking province that it is today, if we consider only its white inhabitants.

Dick King is today a hero, and some English-speaking people would like to see his ride re-enacted every May 25, just as the Afrikaners re-enact the Great Trek. But the truth is that English-speaking South Africans are not capable of emulating the Afrikaners' commemorative fervor.

I do not, however, ask you American young people to take sides in these matters, nor to judge between the British and the Dutch. We have such judges in abundance already. I wish only to show you, how even after the Great Trek, their interests conflicted; and how the Voortrekkers, in their attempt to find a country where they could be free, continually encountered the greater strength of Britain. This will enable you to understand more clearly the South Africa of today.

Indeed in the interior, after the Great Trek, relations between British and Dutch began to improve, and might have gone on improving, if Mr. Trader O'Reilly had not seen the pretty *Orange River stone* at the home of Mr. van Niekerk in 1866, in the dry country near Kimberley. The Afrikaner Republic of the Orange Free State claimed this area, under the Bloemfontein Convention of 1854 by which the British guaranteed the independence of the country between the Orange and the Vaal. But a Griqua chief named Waterboer also claimed the area, and when he applied to the British for protection they annexed the territory. In 1876, in the light of further evidence, the British paid the Orange Free State an amount of £90,000 in compensation, but the damage had been done.

Meanwhile the other Afrikaner Republic, the Transvaal, almost bankrupt, was seriously threatened with Kaffir Wars. With this as reason, but no doubt with the further intention of achieving the unification of South Africa under the Union Jack, the British annexed the Transvaal in 1877. This step not only further antagonized Afrikaner opinion in both Republics, but also many Afrikaners who had remained in the Cape Colony. Slowly but surely the British Government was uniting such opinion throughout South Africa; it was about this time indeed that the unifying name of Afrikaner, as distinct from Transvaaler, Free Stater, and Cape Colonial, began to come more and more into use. In 1880 the Transvaal burghers rose; the British suffered a severe defeat at Majuba, which is another event that remains forever green in Afrikaner history. In 1881 the war ended without victory; self-government was restored to the Transvaal, but in foreign affairs it was to be subject to the Queen's suzerainty. Swaziland was made independent of the Republic, and brought under British protection. But the burghers wanted complete independence, and they were led by Paul Kruger, whom in 1883 they made their President.

The next great event to hit South Africa was the discovery of gold on the Witwatersrand in 1886. Cecil Rhodes already controlled the Diamond Fields; he was now a millionaire, and had great dreams of an all-British route from Cape to Cairo, and of the unification of South Africa under the Union Jack. But Kruger stood in his way; therefore Rhodes sought to contain and confine the Transvaal Republic. He became Prime Minister of the Cape Colony, brought about the annexation of Bechuanaland, and the establishment of the new country of Rhodesia. So with Mozambique to the east, and Natal to the south, Kruger was contained.

Then Rhodes turned his attention to the Witwatersrand itself, where he had great financial interests. Into Johannesburg had poured thousands of immigrants, called Uitlanders by the outnumbered Boers; Kruger altered the voting qualifications to prevent the immigrants from securing control. There was great dissatisfaction, and Rhodes meant to use it. His friend Jameson crossed the border from Rhodesia into the Transvaal with five hundred men, in the famous Jameson Raid of 1895. Rhodes was not ready, there was no answering insurrection in Johannesburg, and the raid failed. But no one had any doubt as to what was now afoot.

That was the end of the influence of Cecil Rhodes in South Africa; every Afrikaner Nationalist loathed his name, and Afrikaner Nationalism grew apace. He was a great man with great ideas; he controlled Kimberley at twenty-seven, built great houses, bought great farms, became a Prime Minister, gave his name to a country, left his wealth to the people, and chose for himself one of the grandest burial places in the world. Yet although he is conventionally remembered, especially on ceremonial occasions in Rhodesia, and although he expected to be remembered for four thousand years, in some strange way he is not remembered at all. That is not because of the Jameson Raid, but because of the strange moral lack in him that permitted the Jameson Raid. He believed in the saying, which has tempted great men throughout history to destruction, that *the end justifies the means.*

Kruger, encouraged by the failure of the raid, now took a stronger line with the Uitlanders. But the British Government sent out an opponent harder and colder than Rhodes, namely Lord Milner. That he must bear a great part of the blame for what followed, is clear from his papers, which are published for all to read.

In October 1899 the Republics declared war on Britain. This was the Boer War, the Anglo-Boer War, the *Vryheidsoorlog* or War of

Freedom. It was called a "gentleman's war," and was generally free of brutality and atrocity. But the British Government pursued a "scorched earth" policy; it burned the farms and put women and children into concentration camps, where over twenty thousand of them died, mostly because of insanitary conditions that were improved when the rising toll of deaths shocked the military into action. This is another of the tragic events of the Century of Wrong, that is freshly remembered, that seems likely never to be forgotten, that even today is argued about by correspondents to the newspapers, in angry and bitter terms.

The war could end only one way, and on May 31, 1902, the Treaty of Vereeniging was signed. The two republics of the Orange Free State and the Transvaal became British colonies, the Orange Free State now being known as the Orange River Colony. The unification of South Africa was thus brought nearer, but its two white races had never been further apart.

17. OUR MODERN HISTORY

After the Anglo-Boer War, there was a period of energetic reconstruction, in which the Governor of the two new Colonies, Lord Milner, played an outstanding and admirable part. But he was an autocrat, and entertained the foolish plan of anglicizing the Boer population. Luckily there were great-minded men in Britain and South Africa at this time. In 1905 Campbell-Bannerman and the Liberal Party came into power in Britain, and in 1906 restored self-government to the Transvaal, and in 1907 to the Orange River Colony. The first Prime Minister of the Transvaal was the Boer General Louis Botha, with the Boer General Smuts as Secretary of State. The first Prime Minister of the Orange River Colony was Mr. Abraham Fischer,

with the Boer General Hertzog as his Attorney-General. English was
to be the official language, but Dutch could be freely used in debates.
The vote was limited to European adult males in these two colonies.

The importance of these events could hardly be overestimated.
They marked the end of British Imperialism. The British Empire
was to undergo great changes, but we must not forget that these
changes took place not only outside Britain, but also within it. Once
give self-government, and you can no longer decide the turn of events.
When the child grows up, the parents must take away their hands
from him. It seems probable that Empire, like slavery, having died
as an idea in the mind, has gone forever.

In 1910 all four colonies formed the Union of South Africa, and its
first Prime Minister was General Louis Botha. Racial conciliation
was in the air. The English and Dutch languages were declared equal.
A wave of goodwill spread over the country. The Cape of Good Hope,
which in 1853 had achieved self-government, had a non-racial franchise, and several thousands of Cape Colored and African voters; this
franchise was to be preserved, but not to be extended to the other
three provinces of the Union. Further, it could only be altered by a
two-thirds majority of both Houses sitting together. These conditions
were not secured, as many Afrikaner Nationalists suppose today, by
the intervention of the British Government, but by representatives of
the Cape Colony itself. All four colonies agreed, however, that whatever the voting rights of nonwhite people, no nonwhite person might
be elected to either House of Parliament. And lastly, on the insistence
of the rural areas of the Cape and Free State, it was agreed that a
rural constituency might be underloaded up to fifteen per cent, and
an urban one overloaded up to fifteen per cent. This had far-reaching
consequences in later years.

But although there was much talk of brotherhood and reconciliation
between the white races, there were large numbers of Afrikaner Nationalists who would have nothing to do with it. They were too near
to the events of the Century of Wrong. They welcomed the recogni-

tion of Dutch, but they wanted rather the recognition of Afrikaans. Jealously they guarded everything that was peculiar to themselves, knowing the dangers of an alien culture; for were there not Afrikaners in the Cape who had become more English than the English?

Afrikaner Nationalism worked openly and boldly for political supremacy. After all, Afrikaners outnumbered English-speaking South Africans, and if only they could be made Nationalists, if only they would use properly the franchise now restored to them, if only they would rebuild their own and not be misled by soft words, then one day they would not only win back the old Republics, but would establish the new Republic of South Africa. Then would Afrikanerdom be triumphant, and South Africa would truly belong to those who had suffered for her so greatly.

The Nationalists now set out to accomplish this task. In 1912 General Hertzog broke away from General Botha, and formed the small Nationalist Party. In 1914 came the First World War, and General Botha took South Africa into it at the side of Great Britain; but much of Afrikaans-speaking South Africa would have nothing to do with a "British" war. Some rebelled; one named Jopie Fourie was shot as a traitor, and he, too, went to join the ranks of the martyrs of Slagter's Nek.

In 1924 the Nationalists under General Hertzog, aided by a small largely English-speaking Labor Party, captured the Government. One of their first acts was to establish Afrikaans as equal with English. Another was to get away from the hated Union Jack, and to have a Union Flag; this was bitterly opposed by English-speaking South Africa, and the present compromise we know. Another important event was when the British Parliament passed the Statute of Westminster in 1931, declaring the absolute equality of status of all Dominions within the British Commonwealth of Nations, which were united only by their common allegiance to the Crown. South Africa thus became the equal of Great Britain and the mistress of her own destinies.

English-speaking South Africa, which after Botha's death, had given almost full support to Smuts, was relieved when Hertzog and Smuts joined in 1933, in the United Party. But a small number of Nationalists again stood aloof, this time under Dr. Malan.

In 1936 Hertzog obtained the necessary two-thirds majority for the transfer of all *African* voters to a separate roll. Eleven members out of 150 opposed the change. In 1938 "Die Stem van Suid-afrika" became a national anthem alongside of "God Save the King."

In 1939 came the Second World War. Hertzog and Smuts differed violently, but Smuts with a majority of thirteen votes again led South Africa into war at the side of Great Britain. Hertzog was reunited with Malan and the Nationalists, but soon after died. There was no rebellion; very many Afrikaners joined the forces, but on the whole the Dutch Reformed Churches, the Afrikaner cultural societies, the Afrikaans-medium schools, the Universities of Stellenbosch, Bloemfontein, Potchefstroom, and Pretoria, stood quite aloof.

Smuts and his United Party came victoriously through the war, but were defeated by the Nationalists in 1948. This was the first all-Afrikaner Government in South Africa; it held the majority of seats, but owing to the underloading and overloading mentioned above, it did so by a minority of votes.

How did the Nationalists finally get in? Who put them in? There is no doubt, that with important exceptions, they were put in by the Afrikaner people. There is no doubt that at no time in their long history had so many of the Afrikaners thought as one. After forty years of Union, during which there had been a minimum of brawling, public and private fighting, and violence, the English-speaking and the Afrikaans-speaking South Africans had never been so divided.

And why did they get in? There is no doubt that they got in because they promised to solve the racial problems of the Union in the traditional Boer way, by the methods of separation or *apartheid;* that is, by separating the races in schools, universities, residential areas, occupations and professions, trains and buses, entrances and exits, libraries, halls, and in every other desirable way. At last the Afrikaner people had a chance to make good the wrong turning that history had taken when the British and their missionaries came to the Cape, and to reassert the supremacy of the white man. In the words of the *Grondwet,* the Constitution, of the Transvaal Republic, there was to be "no equality in Church or State."

I must add that the Afrikaner Nationalists got in again in 1953; and thanks to the overloading and underloading, of which I have already told you, they won thirty more seats than their opponents with a lesser number of votes. With their plans to bring about racial separation, with all the laws they have made and the laws they still intend to make, we must deal later. As far as one can see, Afrikaner Nationalism now has South Africa firmly in its power; as far as one can see, English-speaking South Africans will have to see many of the institutions brought here by the British, changed or abolished; as far as one can see, South Africa is on its way to become a modernized Afrikaner version of the Transvaal Republic. All this should teach us one great lesson, that one cannot govern by suppression if one claims to be a civilized nation. To suppress one must be ruthless, to civilize or to be civilized one must be humane. It is impossible to be both these things at one and the same time. Have the Afrikaners themselves learned these lessons that they taught so well to their conquerors?

It is very important that the Afrikaners should have learned these lessons, for they live in a continent that is awakening from a long period of quiescence. So far we have considered two actors in this great drama, the Afrikaner and the Englishman. But the third actor is waking up. So far the African has been watching the struggle between the others. Now it appears that he will assume one of the leading roles.

Before we consider such important questions, I think we should see more of the country and its people. Meanwhile it is time to take a rest from these studious labors, and to pay a flying visit to that great wonder of nature, the Victoria Falls. Remember, it does not belong to the Union of South Africa; it stretches over a mile between the countries of Northern and Southern Rhodesia. Yet in another way it belongs to all of us, being reckoned by many to be the greatest waterfall in all the earth.

18. THE SMOKE THAT THUNDERS

Our flight from Johannesburg to Livingstone takes about three hours. The farther we fly from Johannesburg, the more undeveloped appears the country below us. We land at the modern airport of Livingstone with a pleasurable feeling of excitement, and cars are waiting for us. At a suitable spot in the middle of the African bush, the cars stop for no apparent reason. But this is so that we can listen to the thunder of the Falls, which are some seven miles away, and so that we can see the great pillars of spray that stand day and night above them.

Above the Falls the Zambesi is a green, mile-wide river, studded with many islands, rich in tropical vegetation. One sails along peaceful reaches, which give no hint of what lies ahead. Crocodiles lie sleeping on spits of sand, and the air is alive with birds. Then suddenly the river quickens, preparing itself for the great business at hand. The Falls differ from most of the waterfalls of Africa in that they do not fall over an escarpment. They plunge into a deep narrow fissure in the earth, so that the mile-wide river is suddenly confined in a narrow gorge whose precipitous sides are at right angles to the direction of the stream. The geological fault is of such a nature that the gorge is zigzag in shape, and keeps on turning at angles of almost 180 degrees, or almost half circle. Thus the river is forced to run first in this direction, and then in that, and changes course abruptly no less than four times in the first mile alone, continuing to do so for some forty miles, when it last emerges into flatter country.

Therefore it is possible to stand on one side of the fissure and to watch the great river plunge over the other. But the volume of spray is so great that at many points one must be content to listen to the thunder of the water, and to see the fall only with the eyes of imagination. At the height of the rainy season the volume of water is twenty times as great as in the driest months, and at these times it is harder than ever to see the fall. At many points on the spectators' side of the fissure, the spray rains down incessantly, sometimes in fine showers, sometimes in torrents; one must go suitably dressed for such weather. As a result of this incessant rain, there is what is called a Rain Forest on this side of this fissure. One of the most interesting things of all to the observer of nature is to move a short distance out of the luxuriant vegetation of the Rain Forest, and to find himself again in the African bush of thorn and baobab, the dry and harsh country of which we saw so much in the Kruger National Park. Elephants are sometimes seen here, and one is asked to avoid them as they can be dangerous. A pedestrian is advised to carry a stick; that is in case he should meet a snake.

The mean height of the Falls is over three hundred feet, but it is only in the driest season and only in certain places that one can see to the bottom of them. But better not to try it at all, for the edge of the chasm is slippery and precipitous, and more than one person has lost his life there. Owing to the incessant spray, the air is full of rainbows, and here also, on suitable nights, may be seen that rare thing, the lunar rainbow.

If we go to the Southern Rhodesian bank of the river, we can see the Devil's Cataract, which by itself and in some other place would be a magnificent waterfall. Here one can see that a new chasm is in process of formation, so that one day there may be a new Victoria Falls, and the old Falls will be part of the gorge; for it is believed that each of the zigzag gorges has had its period of glory, seen by what eyes I do not know.

The Africans of this region call the Falls *Mosi-oa-Tunya,* or the Smoke that Thunders. The first white man to have seen them was the great missionary and explorer, David Livingstone, in the year 1855.

His statue stands on the Southern Rhodesian bank, and it is of course his name that is given to the Northern Rhodesian town where our plane landed. Livingstone was one of the very greatest of the explorers, and, like so many other explorers, wrote of his travels in English of magnificent simplicity; he named the Falls in honor of the Queen.

The Falls are today much as they were when Livingstone first saw them. Man is capable of spoiling much of nature's beauty, but it seems that this place is safe. It is true that a great rail and road cantilever bridge spans the gorge just below the Falls, joining Northern and Southern Rhodesia; but it adds to rather than detracts from the beauty of the scene, and enables us to visit every part of the Falls.

It is my impression that so long as one is in the vicinity of these Falls, they dominate the world. Everyone here is watching them or listening to them, or is thinking about them, or is just enjoying being near them. People eating food are enjoying eating food near them, and even people playing the radio are enjoying playing the radio near them.

I cannot close without quoting one passage from a book by one of the early travelers, James Chapman. Chapman saw the Falls not long after Livingstone, and found them an awe-inspiring sight. He was astonished to find on the very edge of the chasm, and even over it where that was possible, the spoors of elephant, rhinoceros, buffalo, and hippopotamus.

It makes one's hair stand on end to see the numerous indications of their midnight rambles on the very verge of eternity. Here they come at the dead, dark midnight hours to drink the spray and wallow in the mire; and on my asking a native how it was they were not afraid, he asked me in return: didn't they grow up together?

19. DOWN TO NATAL

It is a fine winter's morning for our automobile journey from Johannesburg to Durban. It is cold and fresh, but there is no cloud in the sky, which means that we shall have a warm and pleasant day.

Someone tells us, "You will enjoy the journey, the road is tarred all the way." You will often hear that sentence in South Africa. We are proud of the fact that a road runs five hundred miles, and is tarred all the way. We are very proud of the national road from Cape Town to Louis Trichardt, both of which places you know; this road is twelve hundred miles long, and is tarred almost for its entire length. I suppose we have a right to be proud of it, for such roads are to be found nowhere else in Africa. Soon the national road from Durban to Cape Town, one thousand miles long, will also be completed. That means that for most of the long journeys of South Africa, a very considerable portion can be done on good, weather-proof roads.

The first few miles from Johannesburg are, as you would expect, congested and confusing. But ten miles out of the city we are unmistakably on the highveld again. The road opens out before us in long straight stretches, the countryside is richer and more interesting than the Western Transvaal, and has been well wooded by man. The farms look prosperous, and some fine farmhouses can be seen.

We travel thirty miles to Heidelberg, and at last leave the mines and the mine dumps behind. We then travel seventy miles through this pleasant grass country to Standerton, where we renew fleetingly our acquaintance with the Vaal River. We continue fifty miles to Volksrust, and are about to leave the Transvaal and enter Natal. These three towns, Heidelberg, Standerton, and Volksrust, are typical of interior towns where the Afrikaans influence is supreme; the main Dutch Reformed Church is always a striking building, and often dominates the town.

It will also add to your understanding of South Africa if we consider the population figures, with which I would not otherwise burden you. Once we leave Johannesburg and its environs, where live a million people, we pass Heidelberg at 30 miles (population 7,000), Standerton at 100 miles (population 12,000), and Volksrust at 150 miles (population 7,000). No wonder that the veld seems wide and empty.

We leave Volksrust, travel a few miles, and then suddenly go over the escarpment into the Province of Natal. It is a magnificent view that stretches out before us. By this evening we shall have dropped over five thousand feet, and will be on the warm shores of the Indian Ocean, where winter never comes. But to reach the sea we must traverse this endless panorama of mountain, valley, river, and hill, that is revealed below us.

Up above us on our right is the mountain of *Majuba,* the Place of Doves, where the defeat of the British in 1881 is still celebrated by those who like to. This country through which we are about to pass was the scene of much fighting in the Second Anglo-Boer War, and if you keep your eyes open, you will see many monuments and memorials to those who lost their lives.

We pass through Newcastle (population 12,000) and travel sixty-three miles to Ladysmith (17,000), with the wall of the Drakensberg on our right. Ladysmith was the scene of the famous siege where the Boer forces penned up the British, and delayed their advance into the Transvaal. In this town there is a beautiful Anglican church, with many stained-glass memorial windows and marble tablets bearing the names of 3,200 men who fell during the siege. Away on the right the Drakensberg now rises to heights of over ten thousand feet. It is five thousand feet above the surrounding country, and is wild and magnificent, the greatest mountain mass in Southern Africa. At this time of the year the heights of the mountains are often covered with snow, which is otherwise a rare sight in Africa. From Ladysmith we travel eighteen miles to Colenso (3,000) and twenty miles to Estcourt (7,000), and are now entering that part of South Africa where the

English-speaking influence is strongest.

Here the country changes again in character; this is one of the love-liest parts of South Africa, and gives to Natal the name of the Garden Province. Although the beauty of vastness and space is seen again and again as we drop continuously to the sea, there is now a local beauty of hill and valley, tree and field, which is seldom seen in the interior. The farms are smaller, and signs of human habitation more frequent. The journey is a continuous delight.

When we reach Hilton Road, we are obviously on the edge of another escarpment. For the sake of simplicity I have not previously explained that the escarpment of the great interior plateau drops in steps to the sea. But here it is clearly to be seen. A vast stretch of country lies below us. We see the city of Pietermaritzburg stretched out below us, and beyond it many flat-topped mountains, the largest of which is another Table Mountain, which keeps guard over the famous Valley of a Thousand Hills. This is one of the most magnificent views in Africa. We drop down steeply to the city below (80,000 people).

By many people the city of Pietermaritzburg is regarded as the most beautiful in South Africa. It is the seat of the University of Natal, and has many splendid schools. It is named after two of the Voortrek-kers, Pieter Retief and Gert Maritz, and here is the Church of the Vow, which was built according to the promise made before the Battle of Blood River. But now Pietermaritzburg is largely an English-speaking city, though the growth of the South African Railways and other public services, has brought an increasing number of Afrikaners to live there. By English-speaking people it is called Pieter*mar*itzburg, by Afrikaners Pietermar*itz*burg. But the Zulus call it umGungundhlovu, which is The Place of the Elephant.

Here in the streets we see many Indian people, and on the way to Durban we shall see many more. By many white people they are re-garded as a danger to white civilization, and we shall meet some of them, and learn how they came to South Africa.

We leave Pietermaritzburg, which is fifty-six miles from Durban.

We now no longer see the Drakensberg, but on our left we continue to get many magnificent views of the Valley of a Thousand Hills. The Valley is a large native reserve, and is inhabited by Zulu-speaking people. It is called a reserve because no white person may live there unless with special permission. The old main highway runs on the edge of the Valley, and therefore we shall see many of its people who have come up to buy at the stores, or to catch buses to Pietermaritzburg or Durban.

Some of these people wear Western clothing, but others, mostly women, still wear tribal clothes; or to put it more accurately, they wear a modern version of tribal clothes. They are fond of colored cloths, even colored towels, and like them to contrast vividly with one another. Sometimes the hair of a married woman is piled high up on her head and dressed with reddish clay, presenting a striking sight. Girls and women of all ages frequently wear nothing above the waist, but equally frequently they wear white vests. Sometimes they wear European clothes; these again may have been purchased new, but they may well have been given or sold by some European woman. Most of these African people travel barefoot, over rocks, stones, and thorns; the soles of their feet are hard and tough. In colder parts of the country their feet often crack open in the winter, and if the people are insufficiently nourished, these painful afflictions are very stubborn to heal.

Beads play a great part in their tribal dress, in the shape of necklaces, head circlets, and bangles round legs and arms, even round the waist. These beads are of many colors, and were sold by the earliest traders to come to South Africa, soon replacing the less striking beads in use. The patterns of beads are many indeed, some of them having meanings as clear as those conveyed by words; indeed by the use of beads, and by the use of symbolism, lovers could convey their meanings one to another. Nowadays many Zulus no longer know these meanings.

We stop at one of several points of vantage, and look out over the great panorama of the Valley. It is indeed a Valley of a Thousand

Hills. It is full of rivers and streams, and the calls of many tropical birds can be recognized by those who know them. The central river is the Umgeni, which flows into the Indian Ocean at Durban.

The whole great Valley is an example of erosion caused by many rivers. When Nature had finished her task of making scenery, she began to manufacture a cover and protection for the earth. But now unfortunately Man continues the process of erosion. This is regrettably true of most of the reserves of the Union; let me explain again that a reserve is a tract of land which governments have from time to time set aside for the exclusive occupation of native African people.

Zululand and the Transkei are two notable examples of reserves; perhaps because of their great size, perhaps because of their distance from the great cities, Zululand and the Transkei can still show much of the fascinating interest and beauty of tribal life. Here you will see in actuality some of the beauties of the Duggan-Cronin Bantu Gallery which you visited in Kimberley.

The Valley of a Thousand Hills is nevertheless of great interest to the visitor. It is so near the growing city of Durban that the impact of Western Civilization upon tribal life is clearly to be seen. Special tours are arranged for visitors into the Valley, and these tours are very interesting. Everything will be strange and exciting for the tourist, but he must not believe that he is looking at tribal life. However, the deeper he goes into the reserve, the more nearly he will be able to recapture the past.

One cannot dwell too much or too often on the tremendous impact of Western Civilization upon tribal life. I desire to draw no comparisons between the two, in favor of one or of the other. I merely wish to state that for good or for ill, no tribal culture, no tribal system of law and custom, no tribal habit of dress, no tribal habit of food, no tribal education, can stand beside Western, Christian, industrial, technical, civilization, without withering away.

To Africa the white man brought his ships, his beads and his axes, his guns and his government, his liquors and his foods, his religions and his ideals, his churches and his schools, his books and newspapers, his roads and bridges and radios and cars and airplanes, his doctors and his nurses and his hospitals. There were good things and bad things, but all of them were powerful. They began to work like a ferment, which today is at its greatest.

The great political problem of South Africa today is what to do about this process. Are the Africans to be encouraged to assimilate more and more of this culture? Are they then to be encouraged to enter fully into the political life of this society? What will happen to the white people of the country who are outnumbered by almost four to one? Will the black people of the country subject the white people to a race-domination? Will they do this because they feel that they themselves have been subjected to a race-domination? Are they ready for such political rights? Should they be given some other kind of rights?

These are the many questions that are asked. To these questions there are many answers, but I propose to give them to you at the close of your South African journey.

In the meantime let us stop for a moment on the main road at Inchanga, by this group of African people waiting for the bus. Let me pretend that I know them, and let me tell you what they are and what they do.

The woman there in European clothes, who carries gloves and a handbag, is a trained African sister. She is a member of the Anglican (Episcopal) Church; she is intelligent and capable, with a high standard of personal conduct. She earns about thirty pounds (eighty-four dollars) per month, a high figure for an African woman.

Next to her is a girl in tribal dress. Because she is going to Durban, she wears a little more than usual. She does day labor, weeding and the like, for which she is paid half-a-crown (thirty-five cents) a day. She cannot read or write, and is very simple and childlike in her ways; but she, too, has a high standard of personal conduct. She has never been to school, and is not a Christian.

The man in uniform is a truck driver. He has been to school as far as Standard VIII, but speaks an English far beyond that standard. He reads the newspapers and knows what is happening in the world. He earns about nine dollars per week, but thinks he would get more if he were not black. He is usually smiling, but his concealed resentment sometimes shows itself. He is a member of the Methodist Church.

The truck driver has his son with him, a boy of twelve. The boy is going to be educated as far as his father can take him. Whatever the new world is like, this boy must be ready to take a part in it, a part that his father hopes will be second to none.

The other man there is a humble peasant farmer. He uses terms of great respect to white people, calling them "master" and "lord." He has never had any education. He watches with dismay the decay of the tribal order, but is at a loss to understand what is happening. He is not a good farmer, and his small piece of land is badly eroded. This however is largely due to the fact that his land is on the steep slope of a hill, and in some other country it would not be ploughed at all. This man is not a Christian.

The small girl is thirteen years old. She has reached Standard III, but her parents have decided that it is time for her to work. She is a Christian, speaks simple English, and wears European clothes. She is a simple child, and accepts this early end to her schooling without question. She is obedient to her parents, and respectful to her elders, two striking characteristics of the old tribal society. Her first wage will be about thirty shillings (four dollars) a month, but she will get free food and accommodation.

This man is a day laborer, performing what is called unskilled labor. He cannot read or write, he is not a Christian, and his children do not go to school. His clothes are dirty, and he spends much of his money, and most of his week ends in drinking. The staple drink of the tribal society was a kind of beer, but today powerful and harmful drinks are common. Native Africans cannot buy European liquors such as brandy, whisky, gin, wines, and beers. Therefore the African who wants strong drinks either buys illicitly through some European, Indian, or colored person, or he brews his own harmful liquors. Strong liquor is one of the curses of African life today.

So you will see how different from one another are these people from a reserve. You will see how some have adapted themselves to the Western world with great success, and how others appear not to have adapted themselves at all. Yet not one of them is untouched.

It is time to resume our journey. We leave Inchanga and travel through a very beautiful countryside to Pinetown. Here is still a further fall to the coast. The vegetation becomes more tropical. We see fields of bananas and pineapples; there are pawpaw trees, mango trees, litchi trees; also the avocado pear, often called in America the alligator pear. The gardens are full of the vivid and barbaric colors of poinsettia and bougainvillea. Orange sheets of the golden shower (*Bignonia venusta*) hang from roofs and pergolas. Another magnificent tree, the kaffir boom, is just starting to put forth its blood-red blooms. Two of the loveliest trees of all, the jacaranda and the flamboyant, we shall unfortunately not see in bloom, but they are beautiful trees in any season. Like the jacaranda the flamboyant comes from outside Africa; like the jacaranda it is prodigal with blossom; like the jacaranda it carpets the roadways, though with scarlet, not with blue. Another striking flowering tree is the spathodea, the African Flame, with masses of great orange-red bell-shaped blooms. All these trees and shrubs we shall see in profusion in Durban, where they line the streets and fill the gardens, making this city, for many, one of the most fascinating and beautiful in the world.

We are now on the magnificent highway leading to Durban. We see an increasingly large number of Indian people, the men, boys, and girls in European dress, but most of the women in the colorful costumes of the East. The highway presents a striking sight with its wayfarers of three continents.

Here we are at Toll Gate, on the crest of the ridge known as the Berea. To left and right of us tiled houses look at us through the trees.

Before us is the Bay, one of the finest and busiest harbors in Africa, although its entrance must be kept open by dredgers. Before us also is the "downtown" of Durban, which like the "downtown" of Johannesburg, is strongly reminiscent of any like-sized American city. And beyond all that is the Indian Ocean, blue and sparkling under the sun. Here is the place where winter never comes.

20. THE CITY OF DURBAN

There are many towns of which it could be said that once you had seen one of them, you had seen them all. Durban is not one of them. It is more colorful and luxuriant than the coastal cities to the south, and yet it escapes the extreme heat and lethargy of those to the north.

Its most prominent feature is the Bluff, a long high hill that protects the Bay from the Ocean. This Bluff was first sighted—in recorded history—by Vasco da Gama on Christmas Day, 1497, and he gave the country the name of Natal. British traders arrived in the 1820's, and set up their huts in the tropical bush, with elephants, hippos, crocodiles, and many other animals for their neighbors.

You will remember that the Voortrekkers trekked over the Drakensberg into Natal, and established their Republic there in 1838; then finally they yielded to the superior power of the British, after Dick King had made his famous ride for reinforcements. Dick King's statue we shall see on the Esplanade of Durban Bay, and we shall also visit the Old Fort, where the British were besieged. After this reverse the Voortrekkers returned over the mountains. As a result of immigration from Britain, Natal became the largely English-speaking province that it is today; Durban is the most English-speaking city of South Africa, yet Europeans in it are outnumbered by both Indians and Africans.

The Indians were first brought to Natal in 1860 to work in the newly established sugar plantations, because the Zulus showed no enthusiasm for this kind of labor. After their periods of contract were over, these Indians were entitled to stay in Natal, and many decided to do so, becoming market gardeners, hawkers, and servants. Indian traders followed them; they opened businesses first in the growing town of Durban, but gradually spread out into the hinterland.

These traders were so successful in their operations that in 1911 the Union Government tried to restrict their competition. As a result of this the Government of India brought immigration to an end.

As Indians began to share in the general prosperity of Natal, which they had helped to create, they began also, like other people, to own enough money to invest in property. Perhaps if some area had been set aside for them, they might have invested their money there. But there was no such area, and they began to buy property in areas which up till then had been occupied solely by Europeans.

The Government of 1927 then proposed to reserve certain areas, but after a Round Table Conference with the Government of India, the proposals were withdrawn.

But similar proposals were brought up again in 1943 and 1946, largely because the white people of Durban demanded it. They passed into law, and the Government of India withdrew its representative from South Africa.

Let me remind you that under the present Nationalist Government of 1954, these proposals have been carried much further, and the whole of South Africa is to be divided up into racial areas, so that it will be impossible for any two people of different races, ie., European, African, Indian, and Colored, to occupy houses in the same area. Perhaps you may remember that this law is called the Group Areas Act. Only in this way, says the Government, will the various races of South Africa ever be able to live together in peace.

This argument was given greater force by an outbreak of Zulu violence against Indians in Durban in 1949. Accusing the Indian traders of exploitation, large numbers of Zulus set fire to shops, homes, and buses, and murdered Indian people. Many of the Indians who suffered were the poorest of the poor. It was a terrible time of anxiety, and revealed great racial divisions. But I must not hide from you the opinion of some observers who thought that the Zulus would as readily have turned against the Europeans if they had had the courage.

Amongst many Europeans there is also a great prejudice against Indians, varying from dislike to hatred. If we turn off West Street, the main street of Durban, we are soon in the Indian city. Here are big wholesale houses, and hundreds of smaller shops. Here is the Indian Market, which is a sight you must not miss. Here are schools and mosques.

If we move a little away from the Indian business center, we come to residential sections that are almost wholly Indian. But these overflow as the population increases; Indians have bought property in other areas, and this causes European resentment.

We must also visit some of the African areas. We must go to Lamontville, which is an example of good housing, and to Cato Manor, which is a shocking place of misery, squalor, and disease. Here in Durban, as in Johannesburg, the influx of Africans into the cities has caused grave housing problems. No one pretends that the problems are easy, but places like Cato Manor are blots upon the name of South Africa. African people come to the cities from the overcrowded and overstocked reserves to look for work. By their labor they have made possible the industrial revolution which is taking place. They deserve something better than this.

As you drive to Lamontville, you will see the great new factories that are drawing this labor to Durban, and you will understand the extent of the industrial revolution.

We now return to the city and go down to the Beach for a swim in the Indian Ocean. The water is warm, even in winter. Sharks are always a danger to swimmers, and there are dangerous currents, but we must bathe in the appointed places, where there are lifesavers on duty, with a wonderful record of service to the public. After the swim we shall visit the Snake Park; here in an enclosed garden are all kinds of snakes, and we lean over the walls and watch them. The attendant is inside the enclosure, and he will handle the snakes for our entertainment.

But the most dangerous snake of all is not kept in the enclosure. This is the black mamba, one of the most venomous snakes in the world. It reaches a length of twelve feet and more, and terrible stories are told of its speed and ferocity. At one time it was common in all the coastal regions of Natal. but luckily it retreats from built-up areas. Its poison attacks the nerves of its victim, and brings about paralysis and death in a few minutes. At the Snake Park the black mambas are kept in glass cases, and remain for hours without moving, while the visitor waits for some sign of life.

The green mamba, the cobras, and the adders are also dangerous snakes. The puff adder is the most repulsive of them all. It does not grow to a great length, perhaps three and a half feet, but it has a tremendous girth, and lacks any sinuous beauty. Its poison attacks the blood, and its bite causes agonizing swellings.

Tomorrow we are going to visit a sugar mill on the North Coast, and to see how sugar is made. We shall travel through miles and miles of cane, covering thousands of hills, and waving in the wind. We shall get some idea of the large number of Indians who live in this part of the world. There are one third of a million Indians in South Africa, and most of them live in Natal.

21. THROUGH A TRIBAL RESERVE

It is time now for us to set out on our return journey to Cape Town. It is a journey of a thousand miles, through some magnificent country. Our journey will be comfortable, for a great part of this thousand miles of road is tarred. Villages are few and far between, and we realize again that the main roads of South Africa are a great achievement of a vast and comparatively empty country.

Our first eighty miles, however, is well populated. This is the famous South Coast of Natal, and seaside resorts are found every one or two miles, rejoicing in Zulu names like Isipingo, Amanzimtoti, Illovo, Umgababa, Ifafa, Umtwalumi, Umtentweni. The sun is bright, the sands golden, the sea blue, the water warm. This is the playground of South Africa, and indeed of our northern neighbors who have no coasts of their own. Here on this road can be seen cars from Southern and Northern Rhodesia, from Mozambique, Kenya, and the Belgian Congo, even sometimes from Nigeria.

At Port Shepstone we turn inland into the rolling hills of Natal, cross the Ingeli Mountains, and soon after enter the Transkei. After passing Kokstad we say goodbye to white man's country, and are in the largest tribal reserve in South Africa. Its area is over sixteen thousand square miles (which is roughly twice the size of New Jersey), and it has a population of one and a quarter million Africans, with some eighteen thousand white people, and some fourteen thousand colored people.

We soon know that we are in another kind of country. We are soon passing thousands of the thatched huts of the Mpondo people; these huts lie amongst the fields, empty now, but in the summer, green with maize and millet. It is a beautiful country, but the signs of soil erosion are frequent and alarming, and are more clearly seen in these winter months when the veld is brown and bare.

Most of these huts now have windows, which is a result of education and European influence. They are in groups called Kraals, and in each Kraal is a man with his wife or wives, and his unmarried children, together with his young married sons and their wives and children.

The Mpondo people are divided into patrilineal clans; that is to say, the children belong to the clan of their father. Some of these clans are several thousand strong, and all the members are regarded as related, and they may not marry inside the clan. A tribe is composed of a group of related clans, and is ruled by a chief.

The Kraal, and not the family as among Western peoples, is the important unit. The head of the Kraal was treated with great respect, but so indeed was any older person; and above all was, of course, the Chief. Custom was obeyed unquestioningly, and the individual was spared many duties of choice and decision that often weigh so heavily upon members of a Western culture. It was this, I think, which gave rise to the strange appearance of self-confidence and docility, of pride and innocence, which is to be seen so often in the eyes and bearing of tribal people, and which has been captured so well by Duggan-Cronin in his photographs. I also think that it is this lessening of individual responsibility which makes laughter and merriment so characteristic of the African communities.

I have often seen tribal women in the reserves, suddenly startled by the sound of a car on the road behind them, go running into the grass of the veld with laughter and enjoyment. But you would never see such a sight in any town or city; for a white person to drive carelessly in a city is to invite resentment, to drive carelessly in a city "location" is to invite violence. To injure someone in a location is to invite death.

Here, too, the children wave to us cheerfully as we pass. They love to call out the letters on our number plates, especially if they are TJ (which letters stand for Transvaal, Johannesburg, and mean the One and Only City to these children who have never seen it). Nothing could be more friendly, more open, than these children's greetings. No one could look more friendly, more open, than they. What a great treasure of good will is here, if only we white South Africans do not let it waste away.

The religion of the Mpondo people is based on a belief in the survival of their ancestors, who have great power to help or to harm the living. Disobedience to parents or authority or custom is punished by the ancestors, who bring down illness or bad luck on the offender. At times of serious illness, of birth, marriage, and death, offerings are made to the ancestors. The head of the Kraal slaughters an ox or goat at the entrance to the cattle fold; he calls on the ancestors by name, and asks their blessing. Some meat is burnt for them, and the rest is eaten by the people.

All this is done in reverent fashion, though not with the Christian or churchly kind of reverence to which we are accustomed. These observances were performed with great humility and simplicity, which are the characteristics of all true religious behavior. This humility and simplicity, as I have told you before, were shown first to one's parents and indeed to all older persons, then to the head of the clan, then to the chief of the tribe, and finally to one's ancestors. God himself, the Creator, was considered by some tribes to be remote from human affairs, and was not prayed to; by other tribes God was merely the Oldest Ancestor, the Ancestor of the tribe itself, and he himself emerged from the reeds of the river at some remote but definite point in history.

When Africans become Christians, and carry this humility and simplicity over into their new religion, then they restore to Christianity one of the great qualities of worship.

Added to this simple religion of the ancestors, is the deep-seated fear of witchcraft, which, when it strikes, can turn these proud people into abject and melancholy creatures. Witchcraft is a weapon in the hands of one's enemies, of the jealous, covetous, and quarrelsome. Bad luck comes, and the witch doctor is called in. He smells out the wrongdoer, who in the old days before the white man's law, was often killed. Even today a person who believes himself bewitched can waste away and die, and no white doctor can help him.

Witchcraft and the belief in it, like all other elements in African culture, is today in the transitional stages. Many Christianized Africans have conquered such fears, but many are still subject to them, and in spite of their faith will consult the witch doctor.

Cattle play an important part in tribal life. *Lobolo,* or the *bride price,* is paid in cattle to the father of the bride. Many of the early missionaries made the mistake of supposing that wives were *purchased* in this manner, but the bride price is something much more important than that. It signifies a contract every bit as important as our own marriages, a contract not between two persons, but between two kinship groups.

Cattle play an important part in the religious life of the Bantu people, and in the worship of the ancestors. It is the cattle fold that is the scene of important religious ceremonies. Because of this importance of cattle, quite apart from their value as providers of milk and meat, it is difficult to get the Bantu people to reduce the overgrazing of their reserves. Educators and administrators do their best, but it is difficult to interfere with this deep and religious custom, especially when so much else is seen to be withering away.

But this simple idyllic life is undergoing great changes. Many of the able-bodied men are away at the mines, many young boys and girls have gone into domestic service in the white homes of the cities. Missions and schools have done much to change habit and custom. The white man's doctors and hospitals command an increasing confidence from people who once relied on the skill, part scientific, part dangerous, of their own medicine men.

Nevertheless, if you have eyes to see, you will note that this vast reserve of the Transkei offers a truer picture of tribal life than the Valley of a Thousand Hills. The reason for this is that the Transkei is remote from any great city.

We pass through the town of Umtata, which has a population of 9,000 people, and is the capital of the Transkeian Territories. These territories are divided into twenty-seven districts, and over each of these presides a white magistrate (there being no nonwhite magistrates in South Africa). Each district has a Native District Council, and these councils send eighty-two representatives to the General Council in Umtata. This General Council is called the Bunga, and it consists of the eighty-two African representatives and the twenty-seven white magistrates. This Bunga controls the domestic affairs of the Transkeian Territories; and outside of these affairs it may also pass resolutions for the consideration of the Government of South Africa.

The proceedings of the Bunga are conducted with considerable dignity. As you might expect after hearing about the way in which the Mpondo society is constructed, with its great obedience towards the head of the clan and the tribal chief, the tribes are represented, not by bright young men seeking fame, but by the chiefs themselves. In a way the chief *is* the tribe, and it would be unthinkable for any other person to represent it, unless he were appointed to do so by the chief himself. Therefore the Bunga is a stately affair, conservative rather than radical, old rather than young, respectful to white authority rather than resentful.

But this same modern civilization that so disturbed the tribal way of life, has also affected the power of the chiefs. Many of the young people, imbued with the political ideas of the West, no longer respect the authority of the chiefs. But while they thus seek a greater political freedom, they at the same time often lose the sense of security that the tribe gave to them. Our Government would like to restore the power of the chiefs, and restore the unity of the tribes. Can this be done? I myself think it is impossible, but it remains one of the most burning and controversial questions facing our country.

No one can doubt that the Bunga offers to Africans an opportunity to take part in the affairs of government. It is the belief of the Government that such self-government should be extended and encouraged. But the real government of South Africa is in the hands of the Parliament of Cape Town. Should more and more opportunity be given to the African people to take part in our Parliamentary Government? The majority of white South Africans fear such a development, because there are (in 1954) eight and a half million Africans and only two and three-quarter million whites. That is why many white people feel that a total territorial separation of white and black is the only possible solution of our difficulties. We must discuss these things further before you leave South Africa.

I must close this account of the Bunga with one famous story of its earlier days. The white Government of South Africa made a suggestion

to the Bunga that a tax should be levied on the people of the Transkeian Territories, so that roads and bridges might be built. One old
chief, whose life had not been lived in a world of roads and bridges,
rose to his feet and said, "This reminds me of a man who had a dog.
The dog said to the man, 'I am hungry.' Thereupon the man cut off
the dog's tail and said, 'Take this and eat.' "

Pondoland is the most beautiful part of the Transkei. Here, as in
Natal, the high land falls to the sea in a confusion of hills, valleys,
kloofs, rivers, and waterfalls, with stretches of evergreen forest, in
which grows the *Calodendron capense,* the Cape chestnut, which in
the summer puts forth a profusion of pink blooms that entirely cover
its crown. These patches of color stand out from the various greens of
the forest, and are most lovely to behold. In these forests live the
louries, one of the larger African birds; if we are lucky we shall see
one in flight; if we are still luckier, we shall see one take to flight, and
will call out in wonder as it unfolds its wings, with hues that no South
African dare set down, for fear his whole story of South Africa should
be thought to be a lie.

In olden days the lion, the elephant, the hippopotamus, all roamed
this country. The hippopotamus lives on in the name of the Umzim-
vubu River, which flows out to the sea at Port St. John's, through a
gateway more majestic than any in Africa; for here the escarpment
contained itself in patience, and kept its last leap for the ocean to see
for itself. Near Qumbu is the Tsitsa Waterfall of three hundred and
eighty feet, and near Lusikisiki are the Magwa Falls, where a stream
falls seven hundred feet into the low country. Lusikisiki is thought by
many to be the most beautiful name in all South Africa, and is said
to reproduce in language the sound of reeds cutting against one another
in the wind.

But alas, we cannot stay here any longer. We push on into Tembu-
land, and soon reach the deep valley of the Great Kei River. Remember that this was one of the river boundaries which figures in the
history of conflict between the white settlers from the South and the

tribes from the North. We have now left the lush country of East Pondoland, and the grass country of the highlands, and are in a drier country of thorn and euphorbia. As we cross the Kei Bridge on the fine new highway just completed, we pass from Transkei to Ciskei, and enter a different world, where we shall visit first the city of East London, with a hundred thousand people, and an important port for the wool trade; then the town of Alice, which we are visiting especially so that you can see the non-European University College of Fort Hare and the famous African school of Lovedale, where we shall find African high-school boys and girls from quite another and different part of the country; then the city of Grahamstown, with 25,000 people, seat of the Rhodes University and the home of many famous South African schools.

All this country through which we are traveling is rich in history, for it was here that the frontier struggles between white man and African were waged a century ago, and it was here that the first British settlers came to seek their future on African soil, in 1820.

If we study the place names, we shall see the evidences of their settlement, such names as Kingwilliamstown, Peddie, Port Alfred, Bathurst, Alice, Fort Beaufort, Adelaide, and Bedford.

There are also evidences of the arrival of German settlers, in that part of the country where Stutterheim is to be found; here are places such as Dohne, Frankfort, Braunschweig, Hanover, Berlin, and Potsdam.

Finally we reach the city of Port Elizabeth, fifth of the Union, greatest wool port, with a quarter of a million people. Here we will see the "location" of New Brighton, which is one of the finest schemes for African housing in South Africa, and one of which the city of Port Elizabeth can be proud.

22. THE MOUNTAIN PASSES OF THE CAPE

Between Port Elizabeth and Cape Town lies one of the most beautiful parts of the world.

Along the coast are found the ports and seaside resorts of Humansdorp, Knysna, and Mossel Bay, and this region lies under the first escarpment of the Outeniquas and the Langeberg.

Behind the mountains lies the plain known as the Little Karroo, and this region lies under the second escarpment of the Groot Zwartbergen (the Great Black Mountains) and the Bokkeveld Mountains. Behind them again is the plain known as the Great Karroo, over which we traveled by train when we went from Cape Town to Johannesburg. And yet again behind this is the Nieuwveld Range, behind which lies the Northern Karroo, or High Veld, on which great plain lies the greater part of the Cape Province, the Orange Free State, and the Transvaal. It is this Nieuwveld Range which, under many names, but notably under the name of the Drakensberg Mountains, is the final and highest escarpment, attaining in Basutoland and Natal heights of 10,000 and 11,000 feet, and forming the main watershed for the country.

You will see that to travel from North to South in this part of South Africa means that you will have to cross, in one fashion or another, these mountain ranges. This you do by mountain passes, and it is these mountain passes that are amongst the most beautiful and exciting things to be seen in South Africa.

Sometimes man has had to assault the mountain boldly, as he did when he made the famous Zwartberg Pass, and was forced to go almost to the very summit. But at other times, by some magic not understood by ordinary folk, a river runs right through the mountain mass, and engineers have made a road along its bed, as they did through Meir-

121

ing's Poort, which is also in the Zwartberg Mountains. *Poort* is an Afrikaans word, and like the English word *portal,* means a gateway or opening.

These passes are of every kind. The Tradouw Pass is magnificent, but succeeds also in some way in being gentle, no doubt because of the greenness and lushness of its vegetation and the profusion of its flowers. The Zwartberg Pass is the most magnificent of all, but is harsh and somber. Most fantastic of all the passes to me is the walled-in Seven Weeks Poort, where a dozen times the traveler cannot see how either river or road will find a way.

Now it is clear that we cannot go crossing and recrossing these mountain ranges forever. In the route I have chosen for you we shall go from Port Elizabeth to Humansdorp, and thence through the Tsitsikama Forest to Knysna. From Knysna we shall turn north through the Knysna Forest, cross the Outeniquas by way of the Prince Alfred Pass to Uniondale, thence to de Rust, go through the Zwartberg Mountains by way of Meiring's Poort to Klaarstroom, and so to Prince Albert. Leaving Prince Albert we shall turn south and recross the Groot Zwartbergen by way of the Zwartberg Pass, and then visit the famous stalactite and stalagmite chambers of the Cango Caves; then recross the Outeniquas by way of the Outeniqua Pass, and drop down to the beautiful town of George. Then by way of Mossel Bay we shall return to Cape Town by less adventurous, though still beautiful, roads, with a few more passes thrown in for good measure.

It is a clear morning when we leave Port Elizabeth, and take the fine highway to Humansdorp, fifty miles away. We are still in the thorn country, but when we pass Humansdorp, we enter a different world, for the Outeniqua range of mountains catches the moisture-laden winds from the ocean, and the whole coastal belt abounds in rivers, streams, forests, and ferns; in the spring it is rich in wild flowers of every kind, and one passes small lakes and pools covered with water lilies, and meadows ablaze with watsonias of every color.

We go through the beautiful Tsitsikama Forest, down steep winding roads through walls of trees and bordered by ferns, bracken, and arum lilies. The giants of the forest are the yellowwoods, and another famous tree is the stinkwood, whose finished timber is very striking, and is much used for furniture making.

We reach the town of Knysna, (population 8,000), and visit the tearoom at the Knysna Heads, where the rollers of the Indian Ocean enter the harbor through a gateway formed by sandstone cliffs. We could stay here for hours, watching the great numbers of sea and water birds, but we must leave soon and take the road into the Outeniqua Mountains. This passes first through the Knysna Forest to Deepwalls, about thirteen miles away. Here is the famous King Edward VII tree, a yellowwood 137 feet high, and said to be 1,700 years old.

We now leave the forest and begin the ascent of the magnificent Prince Alfred's Pass, the first of our great mountain passes. We are hardly over the pass before the country changes from one of forest and fern and wild flower into one of rock and stone; it is the Little Karroo with its own beauty of quite another kind. There is still greenness here, however, especially along the watercourses. So we proceed to de Rust, the small village which lies under the Zwartberg Mountains, and at the entrance to Meiring's Poort.

As we are traveling north, we are running against the direction of the river that flows through the mountains. We are going to drive along-side of it for thirteen miles, and to cross it thirty-two times. At first the scenery is moderately interesting, giving no hint of what is to come. But soon we are entering the mountain itself, and the walls of rock on either side begin to rise higher and higher. They are of many colors, but red is predominant. The whole scene would be harsh and desolate but for the river and the trees, and the many birds that fly about the road. We want to stop at every bend, and to get out and to look up at the cliffs of contorted stone, that now rise to a height of two thousand feet above us. Then, at last, the majestic journey is over, and we emerge into the arid country of the Great Karroo.

We now turn west, and drive under the range to Prince Albert,

(3,000 people), a distance of some forty miles.

You will notice that the names of British royalty figure prominently in these almost entirely Afrikaans-speaking districts. This is a reminder to us that the Cape Colony passed into the hands of the British at the beginning of the nineteenth century.

Here at Prince Albert we are only twenty-eight miles from the main railroad from Cape Town to Johannesburg, along which we traveled when we first started to explore the interior of South Africa.

From Prince Albert we turn south for our second crossing of the Zwartberg Mountains. We travel five miles before we reach the foot of the mountains, and search the towering wall in vain for any way to ascend it; nor is there any sign of any road above us. Then we enter a great crack in the escarpment, down which flows a stream. It is reminiscent of Meiring's Poort, but the walls are closer, and because of that, more fierce and forbidding. We cannot continue like this, because this stream does not cut its way through the mountains like the other.

Then the road leaves the stream and begins the ascent of the wall itself in a series of awesome curves like which there is nothing else in South Africa. This is the Zwartberg Pass, the most magnificent of its kind, and made still more magnificent by the unrelieved harshness of its surroundings.

Then we reach the top, and begin the long descent to the Cango Caves.

These are among the finest limestone caverns in the world, and were first discovered by a farmer who pursued a wounded buck into a small opening in the mountainside. What he thought of them, and whether he was able to see much of them, and whether he ever found the buck, we are not told. Today one can be guided on a two-mile journey through innumerable chambers and corridors, containing some fearful tunnel-like ascents.

The water seeps down continually through the earth and rocks, and, charged with carbonates, reaches the roof of some tremendous chamber, where it falls drop by drop, leaving at its point of fall and at its point of arrival on the stony floor, a microscopic deposit of carbonate. One pillar called the stalactite grows from the ceiling, and another called the stalagmite grows to meet it from the floor, till after centuries they meet. So they form organ pipes, canopied beds, pillared temples, statues, and bridal chambers; forms of animals and men and demons; some white, some tinted with colors from who knows where; all of them fantastic.

When I first visited the Caves, the guide illuminated each treasure with a magnesium flare, but today he turns a switch, and waits for the exclamations of the company.

We leave the Caves and travel to Oudtshoorn, through the Little Karroo, remarking again how even in this world of thorn and rock and stone there are green trees and fields and pleasant farmhouses. The most striking tree is the Lombardy poplar, planted in straight lines, an inescapable feature of the pattern that human beings have imprinted on the Little Karroo.

This part of the world is the center of the ostrich-feather industry, and we shall pass farms where we shall see these great birds. At one time it was the height of fashion for a woman to wear an ostrich plume in her hat, and ostrich farmers were very wealthy. Oudtshoorn was the center of the industry. But those days have gone, and the feather industry is not so rewarding today.

The national road from Oudtshoorn descends the magnificent Outeniqua Pass, and here we leave the Little Karroo and return to the luxuriant coastal region, reaching finally the town of George (12,000 people), which is thought by many to be the loveliest small town in the Union of South Africa.

The whole of the journey from Port Elizabeth to Cape Town via Humansdorp, Knysna, George, Oudtshoorn, Ladismith,* Barrydale, Robertson, Worcester, and Paarl, is usually called the Garden Route. It is impossible to take any one route and to include all the wonderful

---

* Not to be confused with Ladysmith which is in Natal.

sights that are to be seen. We are going to return to Cape Town from George by the more direct route through Mossel Bay, Riversdale, Heidelberg, Swellendam, and Caledon. By so doing we must lose our chance of seeing the Seven Weeks Poort, the Tradouw Pass, the Du Toit's Pass, and the Bain's Kloof Pass. But we shall go out of our way to see the University town of Stellenbosch.

After leaving the attractive seaside town and resort of Mossel Bay we leave the coastal region, and run many miles over the open stretches of heath-covered moors to Heidelberg. We have now left the Outeniquas, and travel along the base of the Lange Berg, which as you may guess, is the Long Mountain, until we reach Swellendam (5,000 people). You will see that we are now passing into a wheat-growing country. Swellendam is one of the oldest towns in South Africa, having been founded in 1747; it contains several old buildings and some lovely old houses, and water flows between the sidewalks and the streets. It has a magnificent mountain background, but we shall now seldom see a town that has not.

We now travel under the Zonderend Mountains to Caledon (4,000 people). Here is another district famous for its wild flowers, and Caledon has its own Wild Flower Park, which is a never-to-be-forgotten sight in the spring months, and attracts tens of thousands of visitors. The town has famous mineral springs, and lies under yet more mountains.

We now approach the Hottentots Holland Mountains, which we often saw when we were in Cape Town, on the other side of False Bay. We do not run under these mountains, for they are a spur of other mountains, and lie athwart our path. We cross them by means of the Sir Lowry Pass, and descend finally to Somerset West, soon branching off the main road to pay our visit to Stellenbosch.

In Stellenbosch, as in Grahamstown, but even more so, the University dominates the town. Princeton is probably the best American parallel to this. If one saw a large building in Stellenbosch, one would be surprised to learn that it was not part of the University. The Uni-

versity has over two thousand students, and although it is smaller than
the Universities of Cape Town and the Witwatersrand, it is the most
famous. One need only mention that of the four Prime Ministers who
have held office since the Union came into being in 1910, three were
Stellenbosch men.

You may guess then that Stellenbosch is an Afrikaans University.
Here the Dictionary of the Afrikaans language is being compiled, and
the Theological Seminary has produced most of the eminent ministers
of the main Dutch Reformed Church.

There is only one thing that equals education and religion in importance at Stellenbosch University, and that is Rugby football.

The town itself is the second oldest in South Africa, yielding place
only to Cape Town itself. It was laid out by Commander van der
Stel in 1679, and was named after him. The streets are lined with oaks,
water runs beside the sidewalks, and there are many beautiful old
houses. And outside the town, under the inevitable mountains, are
the vineyards.

We leave this lovely town and are soon on the undistinguished
stretches of the Cape Flats. But the monotony of this journey is relieved by the sight of more great mountains ahead. They are of course
the mountains of Cape Town itself.

23. THE FUTURE

What is to be the future of the beautiful land of South Africa?
How will its Afrikaners, its Africans, its English-speaking people, its
Indians, its Colored People, be able to live together? Can such happiness be attained only under the leadership of the white man, and
only so long as nonwhite people agree to this leadership? Can such
happiness be attained only when all the races are kept separate from
one another, by franchise laws, marriage laws, transport laws, housing

laws, school laws, cinema laws? If this separation is carried out, will all the facilities remain equal? Can separation with full equality be achieved as many say it can? Or will it be necessary to declare that there can be only one South African Parliament, one South African Railways, one South African Army, one South African Police, one South African Mint, one South African Reserve Bank, and that these and other national organizations must always be controlled, at all important levels, by white persons?

What would happen if one really opened all the doors of opportunity to everybody? Would it mean that the nonwhite people would grasp political power for the purpose of seeking revenge? Would they pass laws that would make life intolerable for white people? In other words, would we pass from white domination to black domination? Or would the whole country be happier, and would people stop thinking in terms of color? And would the price of this happiness be that South Africa would become a "mixed" nation? And is a "mixed" nation degenerate, lazy, and irresponsible?

Suppose that you were a white person who feared black domination. Would you be prepared to defend white domination at all costs, even of your life, even of the life of your people? If you were a white person or a nonwhite person who hated any racial domination, what would you do in a contest of rival nationalisms? Would you leave the country, or turn to gardening? Or would you declare that these rival nationalisms are not such giants as they seem, and should be resisted valiantly?

What is the end to be? Will it come about violently, or is this only alarmist talk? Will it come soon, say before the end of this century, or will it take much longer? Is there plenty of time, or hardly any? Is it possible that there will not be any violence at all, but that the industrial revolution will give nonwhite workers more and more economic power, so that they could paralyze the country if they would? Would they then make political demands that white people would have to agree to? Is this the way change will come?

Or will change come also in the white heart and mind? Will the idea of racial domination become more and more morally intolerable to the very people who hold it in practice? Or will it be seen to be utterly impracticable? The idea of slavery lost its hold on the human mind; will the idea of racial domination lose its hold, too? Could a real crack appear in the white supremacy wall that today looks so massive and solid?

And what about communism? In a country like South Africa, where there is a considerable amount of poverty and squalor, and where people are prevented *by law* from enjoying certain opportunities, what is the future of communism? Do not deprived people readily turn to communism? Do not Communists try to capture all the organizations formed by such people? Do not Communists try especially hard to capture black Nationalist movements? Is there not a danger then that if there were another world conflict, Africa would be the giant Fifth Column of the Communists?

What a terrible list of questions to come after our happy journey through South Africa! Yet these are the questions that we all ask ourselves. Have no fear, I do not intend to answer them all. But I must make some kind of answer, and I intend to do this only in a general way.

Before I do this, let me remind you that I have a strong point of view of my own; therefore you must examine closely all I am going to say. This strong view of my own is at present held by very few white people in South Africa. These few white people reject the ideal of a *separated society,* and uphold the ideal of a *common society.* They do not believe in racial discrimination (or differentiation, which is another name but the same thing to them) by law or authority. They believe that the evils of racial discrimination (or differentiation) are far greater than its benefits. They believe that discrimination, or differentiation, (or segregation, to give it its ugliest name), is always done by someone with power to someone without power, and is fundamentally unjust. They may believe that this goal of a common society must be reached by steps, but they have no doubt what the goal is—a Union of South Africa, united and indivisible, belonging equally to all its people, offering to all its people equal opportunities, rights, and duties, knowing therefore no discrimination whatsoever on the grounds of race and color.

But lots of people do not hold these views at all. I am going to try to tell you what their views are, and what the views are of non-white people also. Let us consider these various beliefs and opinions.

1. White Domination

A large number of white voters know that the future is uncertain. Whatever the dangers, and because of the dangers, they intend white domination to remain; it will be stern, and will be as just as circumstances will permit. They regard any social or other mixing of the races as intolerable, and are strong supporters of racial separation or *apartheid.* However, they regard *total apartheid,* that is a complete territorial separation on the grand scale, as impracticable. The great majority of these voters vote for the Afrikaner Nationalist Party.

2. Total Apartheid

A small but influential number of white voters think that *white domination* is impossible to maintain, for both practical and moral reasons. They believe in *total apartheid,* and are willing to make great sacrifices to attain it; only so, they maintain, will white people overcome their fears and black people receive justice. This influential minority is well supported by Afrikaner intellectuals and church leaders, and most of them vote for the Afrikaner Nationalist Party.

Thus a majority of the party disagrees with a minority on this important question. This has not yet led to any breach in the party. This is because they are all Afrikaner Nationalists who have all fought and stood together to achieve political victory; they feel that there is more to bind them together than to keep them apart.

3. *White Leadership*

Another large number of white voters, as large as the Afrikaner Nationalist Party, does not believe in *total apartheid,* and does not like the public sound of the words *white domination.* These people have therefore evolved a policy which could be called *reasonable apartheid under white leadership.* They support the United Party, and are largely English-speaking. The United Party, being largely English-speaking, is not so subject to the powerful tradition of *apartheid* as the Nationalists. Nevertheless it is equally subject to the racial prejudices of white South Africa. I would describe its policy as cautious and conservative, too much so for the times in which we live.

4. *Common Society*

A small number of white voters hold the same view as myself, namely, that racial discrimination is indefensible, morally and intellectually. We call ourselves Liberals, but many of our opponents call us "liberalists," and this is a term of contempt. Another term of contempt is "kafferboeties," which means the same as the American term "nigger lovers." Sharing these Liberal ideals are also a number of Africans, Indians and Colored People, how many no one can say.

5. *Communism*

There is also a small number of white voters who are Communists or near-Communists. They are not openly so because, under the Suppression of Communism Act, there are heavy penalties attached to the propagation of Communist ideals and ideas. They also are against any kind of racial discrimination, but in addition they have pronounced ideas about social organization, ownership of land, industry, mineral wealth, and so forth. They, too, share their ideals with a number of Africans, Indians, and Colored People, and some have endured suffering and material loss for the sake of their beliefs.

6. African National Congress

The largest African organization is the African National Congress. How powerful this body is, no one can say. The Government has done great damage to the Congress by "banning" many of its prominent members; a leader of the Congress can be ordered not to stir from his immediate neighborhood for a year or more, or to refrain from attending any meetings. A leader can be "banned" by the Government by a mere letter of notice; there is no trial, no conviction, no appeal. Will such measures intimidate the Congress, or strengthen its resolution? Answer, *nobody knows.*

Some of the leaders of the Congress are Communists. Some have been "banned." Some of these banned have not been Communists. The African National Congress has not declared for or against communism. It says that its main struggle is against Racial Discrimination, and it welcomes all who are against such discrimination.

The President of the Congress said to me, "On my left is a man who fights with me the cause of the African people. On my right is another. How can I dream of asking either of them his views on lesser politics?"

That is the real truth about communism in the African National Congress. In the present situation it is regarded as "lesser politics."

What is the truth about Nationalism, African Nationalism, in the Congress? African leaders declare that the Congress is for all South Africa, not just for Africans. They are utterly opposed to *apartheid.*

Are these democratic declarations true? I am sure many of them are. Will they always be true? Answer, *nobody knows.*

7. Indian Congress

The largest Indian organization is the Indian Congress. The Government has also done great damage to this Congress by "banning." There is also a Communist element in the Indian Congress, but here again no one asks about "lesser politics." The great enemy is Racial Discrimination.

8. Colored People

The largest Colored organization is called the Colored Peoples' Organization. It stands with the two Congresses against all racial discrimination. But the Colored People are not as yet united on this issue. The reason is that they have never been so completely excluded from the white man's society as the Africans and Indians; they hesitate to make common cause therefore with all nonwhite people.

This is a very complicated picture, but I hope that your tour round the Union has helped you to understand it. Now, what of the future?

No one should ever foretell the future. When he is healthy and well, the future looks bright; when he is ill, the future fills him with anxiety. When his own affairs take a turn for the better, he thinks the country's affairs may do the same; but when his own affairs go badly, then he is pessimistic about his country. You will find that people who are pessimistic about their country are very often, though not always, pessimistic about life itself.

Furthermore, it is risky to foretell what is going to happen at any time when one may still be alive. Therefore I am rather going to indicate various possibilities, all of which I think are reasonable. But do not forget that some great event may happen, some great discovery may be made, that may change the face of history, and create an entirely new set of possibilities.

Now, as you know, political power is in the hands of white people. Some stand for white domination, some for *total apartheid*, some for white leadership, some for a common society. Who will win? Or will none of them win? Will the decision be wrested out of their hands? Here are the various possibilities.

1. One thing is certain. Nonwhite opinion will grow in unity and strength. Nonwhite labor will grow more powerful, even though it is not permitted to organize itself lawfully, as is the case today. White people will see this strength, and maybe feel its power. Will they fight it or make peace with it?

More and more will white people have to choose between white domination and the common society. *Total apartheid* will be seen as a fantastic impossibility, and the policy of *white leadership* will be seen as halting between two opinions.

2. Who will win out, the group for white domination, or the group for a common society? If white domination wins, some violence, whether of internal revolution or external interference, must be expected. Domination by a minority is an unstable condition.

3. Suppose those who support the *common society* achieve a majority. Will the common society continue as a true democracy, or will it be followed by *black domination,* the great revenge?

This of course is a possibility, and one that is much feared, but if world opinion is as strongly against any kind of racial domination as it is today, the danger is not so great. This is one of the real questions confronting us, not what kind of country we will be, but what kind of world will we be in.

In any case, white South Africans must be prepared for a great change in their traditional way of life. Such a great change came about in the traditional way of life of the British aristocracy during this century. It came about without violence, even with very little bitterness. But of course it was not a race and color problem.

4. Whatever happens, I do not think that *total apartheid* will ever be much more than a dream. There is not enough land for it; there is not enough time for it; there is not enough money for it. But above all there is no real will for it.

A great question remains. When *total apartheid* is seen to be impossible, what will the Afrikaner intellectuals and religious leaders do? Will they choose white domination or the common society? Surely, with their intellectual qualifications and their moral views, they must choose the *common society*.

What an important thing for South Africa this would be! I cannot think of any more important or more exciting thing that could happen. The danger of revolution would recede. The danger of conflicting nationalisms would recede. Millions of hopeless people in South Africa, both black and white, would begin to look to the future with hope. Millions of people would accept Afrikaner leadership at last. Some white people would hold up their hands in horror, and say, "What will happen to racial purity?" We have a hard lesson to learn, and that is that the enforcement of racial purity by law requires racial domination; and racial domination will bring revolution. In other words, the pursuit of racial purity does not lead to racial peace. Yet many Afrikaner Nationalists suppose this to be the case.

We shall have to learn the same lesson as America, and that is— let a government look first and last to justice, and leave the people to look after other things themselves.

5. Suppose that the most feared of all these possibilities came to be true, namely, an era of violence and revolution? Would communism have played a great part in that? Is communism playing a great part now? Answer, *nobody knows*.

Here is a great struggle of people to be free. They are moving from a tribal to a Western life, but are impeded by many obstacles, some of them man-imposed. No one must underestimate the possibility that communism may capture the African mind. But it appears at the moment that there is a struggle within the African National Congress itself, and that three ideals struggle to possess the African soul. One is the Communist ideal of the triumph of the proletariat, one is the Nationalist ideal of Africa for the Africans, one is the ideal of the Common Society.

One thing is certain, *apartheid* is not one of the ideals that will possess the African mind.

Another thing is certain. Any intelligent white ruling class would exert every effort to extend the ideal of the Common Society.

Otherwise, there will be a revolution concerned only with class or racial goals. It could bring about the world conflict that will end the world.

6. How much time is there to choose between the revolutionary solution and the evolutionary solution? Answer, *nobody knows*. Nobody knows how successful the Government will be in preventing the growth of a common opinion (and of course a common purpose, a common strength, a common resolve) amongst the nonwhite peoples. Perhaps all the time this common resolve is growing. *No one knows how great it is.*

But some sudden event could hasten the growth of this common resolve. Some new law maybe, some new leader maybe, some new event in Africa, could fill all Africans, all nonwhite people, with a new resolve and purpose.

Equally well can it happen that the idea of *domination* will lose its lodgement in the white mind.

In 1960 the massive wall may show a crack.

In 1970 the crack may have become a breach.

In 1980 the waters may be pouring through.

In 2000 the river may be flowing quietly to the sea, with only a few ruins left of its former impediment, to be preserved as historical monuments of the folly of mankind.

This *could* happen. There is very little sign of it now. At present an army of engineers, builders, plasterers, masons, are busy making the wall stronger than it has ever been. This in fact has been the task of our Parliament since the Nationalist Party triumphed in 1948, and it will be the main task for many years to come. Some say it will take 50, 100, 150 years, to bring about the ideal of *total apartheid*.

Let us pay another visit to the Houses of Parliament, and attend one of the important debates. These debates have, since 1948, been largely concerned with *apartheid* legislation, and with the control of Communists and those who "incite racial hostility." There have been bills to remove Colored voters to a separate roll, to limit the rights of the courts to test acts of Parliament, to transfer all African schools from the Education Department to the Native Affairs Department, to divide the whole of South Africa into racial areas where only members of one racial group can live. Note, however, that all white people are regarded for this purpose as belonging to one racial group; but not in the schools—here the Afrikaans-speaking children and English-speaking children are being separated from one another in an increasing measure.

Here in these Houses of Parliament a great social experiment is being conducted. A whole nation is being reconstructed. For many years, the peoples of South Africa have been moving about in an unplanned fashion, from country to town, from farm to factory, from native reserve to city, from the Transkei to Cape Town, from Zululand to Durban, from Sekukuniland to Johannesburg. But now all such movement, all such development, is to be planned, and the purpose of the plan is to keep the various peoples as separate from one another as possible.

Into this planning is going more time, more money, more energy, than have ever been used before in any planning in the Union of South Africa.

It is fantastic to stand before these Houses of Parliament, and to realize that most of this work will be undone. How? Peaceably, we earnestly hope. When? Who knows? But I will venture to predict that the undoing process will be in full swing by the year A.D. 2000.

Will our legislators become famous? Yes, they will become as famous as King Canute.

24. TOT SIENS

Our journey is over now, and I am sorry to part company with you. It has been a great pleasure to me to show you my country.

It is very important to me that young people from other countries (I do not call them foreigners, because I dislike that word) should visit us, and try to understand the difficulties of our problems. Especially am I glad that Americans should visit us. It is very important that Americans should understand the problems of as many countries as possible, because America has such power, and therefore such responsibility, in the world. I believe that America takes her responsibility very seriously, and therefore it is important that she should increase her knowledge.

There may be some mistakes of fact in this book, but the whole picture is for me essentially true. People who disagree with my main conclusions will naturally look for mistakes of fact, so that they can discredit this book. It cannot so easily be discredited. It is written by a South African who was born in South Africa, and feels a high allegiance to his country.

But an allegiance to our own countries becomes deeper and truer when we owe an allegiance to something even greater, to truth, to justice, and to the welfare of the whole human race. That is what I believe, and I know that many Americans believe it too; they believe that that is the way to become not only better citizens of the world, but better citizens of America also. They become better able to carry out their great responsibility to the world.

As your ship leaves the harbor of Table Bay, I say not *goodbye,* but *tot siens,* which means that I hope to see you again. As you sail away from Africa, you will for a long time see the great mass of Table Mountain, the same as was seen by the first white men who came to make their homes in South Africa. They brought a new life to this country. They changed the old life beyond recall. It goes on changing, and it is our duty to see that it changes for the good of all who live here.

No country likes interference from outside in its internal affairs. Yet no country can live without some kind of interference from outside. From now onwards your interest in South Africa should be better informed than it was a few weeks ago. And above all, remember this —the greatest service that any person can render to the cause of peace and justice in the world is to ensure that peace and justice prevail in his own country. Justice in the ideal is a powerful thing, but justice in practice is more powerful still, and can influence powerfully all the peoples of the world.

Tot siens.

INDEX